The Fabled Third

Also by Liam Guilar

Rough Spun to Close Weave
I'll Howl Before You Bury Me
Anhaga
Lady Godiva and Me
A Presentment of Englishry
A Man of Heart

Liam Guilar

The Fabled Third

Part three of
A Presentment of Englishry

Shearsman Books

First published in the United Kingdom in 2025 by
Shearsman Books
PO Box 4239
Swindon
SN3 9FN

Shearsman Books Ltd Registered Office
30–31 St. James Place, Mangotsfield, Bristol BS16 9JB
(this address not for correspondence)

EU AUTHORISED REPRESENTATIVE:
Lightning Source France
1 Av. Johannes Gutenberg, 78310 Maurepas, France
Email: compliance@lightningsource.fr

www.shearsman.com

ISBN 978-1-84861-964-7

Copyright © Liam Guilar, 2025

The right of Liam Guilar to be identified as the author of this work has been asserted by him in accordance with the Copyrights, Designs and Patents Act of 1988.
All rights reserved.

Contents

Introduction and Acknowledgements / 7

Two Stories   11

Chapter One. Gwydion   19
Chapter Two. Uther   29
Chapter Three. Ness   40
Chapter Four. Ygrayne   50
Chapter Five. First Crown Wearing   65
Chapter Six. Dunian   82
Chapter Seven. York   91
Chapter Eight. Second Crown Wearing   108
Chapter Nine. To Tintagel   117
Chapter Ten. Tintagel   131
Chapter Eleven. Pay the Piper   144
Chapter Twelve. The Education of Arthur mab Uthr   151

Laʒamon's Last Interview   162

Do not waver / Into language. Do not waver in it.
         —Seamus Heaney

The story takes us back to an archaic world whose primitive manners lie beyond our sympathy and comprehension. Very little emotion or human response is in any way expressed, and there is a total absence of compassion. No apology or explanation is either given or expected for deeds of unprovoked violence: […] there is a complete lack of moral perspective…

   —Bromwich and Evans, Introduction to *Culhwch and Olwen*.

Introduction and Acknowledgements

The Fabled Third is the final instalment in the sequence that began with *A Presentment of Englishry*. Like the other two books, it follows Laȝamon's 12th century version of the legendary history of Britain. Beginning where *A Man of Heart* finished, with the death, or disappearance, of Vortigern, it tells the story of Uther Pendragon and his struggle to unite the province of Britannia. The sequence ends as it begins to overlap with Sir Thomas Malory's better-known version of the Arthurian story.

All three books tell a story about storytelling. The story of Arthur's conception erupts into the familiar patterns of the *Brut*. It would be at home in *The Mabinogion*, where shape-shifting is commonplace. I have introduced versions of Welsh stories that must have been circulating while Laȝamon was alive. Although I've known and loved them for decades, I didn't feel comfortable rewriting them until after I had translated the originals. The editions I used are given in the footnotes. There is a current fashion for rewriting medieval and classical stories to make them acceptable to an idealised modern audience. I think this is a mistake. No one makes an accurate map of a landscape by removing the features they find objectionable.

When Uther arrives at Tintagel, he doesn't enter the fifth-century settlement revealed by recent archaeology: he enters a castle that didn't exist on the site until after Laȝamon finished writing. Looking at the fifth century through the words of a twelfth-century writer produces a strange version of the past, which has been further distorted by my attempts to reconcile it with what little is now known about the period. I recommend the pleasures of a flexible attitude towards geography, history, architecture and chronology.

A lengthy project like this incurs numerous debts. My thanks to Tony Frazer for publishing the books; to the late Michael Alexander, whose comments on *A Presentment of Englishry* included a pointed reminder that the period wasn't all war, plunder and mayhem, and to Jeremy Hooker, whose comments on *A Man of Heart* came at a time when I didn't think I could finish the third book. I am grateful to everyone who read and commented on drafts of these books, and to those who have answered questions on a bizarre range of topics. Special thanks to Cassie Forster for reading complete drafts of the last two books, and to Josephine Balmer for her patient assistance throughout with matters Classical. Any mistakes are mine.

'The Punishments' and the two translations from *Culhwch and Olwen* appeared in *The High Window*. 'Gwydion' and 'Laȝamon's Last Interview' appeared in *Long Poem Magazine*. My thanks to the editors, especially to the editors of *Long Poem*, Linda Black and Claire Crowther, for their ongoing interest. There are very few print outlets for ten pages of narrative verse.

Nu biddeð Laȝamon alcne æðele mon;
for þene almiten Godd.
þet þeos boc rede; & leornia þeos runan.
þat he þeos soðfeste word; segge to-sumne.
for his fader saule; þa hine forð brouhte.
& for his moder saule; þa hine to monne iber.
& for his awene saule; þat hire þe selre beo. Amen.[1]

---

[1] Laȝamon's *Brut* lines 29-35. Direct quotations from the *Brut* are taken from the University of Michigan's superb *Corpus of Middle English Verse and Prose*: https://quod.lib.umich.edu/c/cme/LayCal.

Two Stories

1 The death of Hengist

Hit befell in the dayes of Uther Pendragon, when he was kynge of all Englond, and so regned, that there was a myghty duke in Cornewaill that helde warre ageynst hym longe tyme, and the duke was called the Duke of Tyntagil. And so by meanes Kynge Uther send for this duk, chargyng hym to brynge his wyf with hym, for she was called a fair lady and a passynge wyse, and her name was called Igrayne.
                    Sir Thomas Malory.[1]

But the story doesn't start there.

It begins:

God but it was cold on the slopes of Dunian.
The scattered survivors of Uther's army
huddled amongst the boulders on the summit
hiding from the wind that tried to flay them.
If the cold didn't crush them in the night,
the Saxons would slaughter them at dawn,
Down there in the valley, those tiny lights,
campfires of an army, taking its time.

It doesn't start there either.

It starts with Hengist striding to his ship,
his children watching him depart.

Or Caesar contemplating glory
and the channel crossing.
Or Locrin, Gwendoline,
Brutus, Aeneas, Helen.
A city burning or a city being built.

---

[1] *Le Morte Darthur*, p.1, edited P.J.C. Field, D.S. Brewer 2017.

But this story, the one we're telling you,
has to start somewhere, so we begin
after Hengist destroyed Gloucester's army
on Salisbury plain. You can read about it
in *A Man of Heart* (Shearsman 2023).
Turning his shambling horde,
he shuffled it north, like a bush fire
destroying everything it touched.

Gorlois finally led his troops across the Tamar,
caught the sprawl of plodding Saxons,
slaughtering the stragglers.
By the time Hengist had wrenched his force around
Gorlois had retreated to an old hill fort.
The Saxons raged against bank and ditch,
but lacking siege equipment
couldn't make their numbers count.

Meanwhile, messengers had found The Boys
and though the brothers argued, Uther lost.
Following Merlin's advice, Aurelius
speared his force into the Saxon host.

With the simple, single-minded focus
of a man who understands one action
might atone for all the mischief
and erase all talk of failures and mistakes
Gloucester hacked his way to Hengist
till face to face, sparks flew, sword biting sword.
Gloucester smashing Hengist's shield
Hengist shattering Gloucester's helmet.
Dazed, staggering, but then the sight
of fresh men streaming down the hill,
with Gorlois at their head, renewed his spirit.
One blow to the hand and Hengist dropped his sword,
grabbed by his mail shirt, thrown down,
swamped by numbers. Gloucester crowing,

incoherently, where's the knife now, dog?
Gorlois at his side, they bind him, dragging him
by his hair before The Boys, with the Britons
spitting on him as he passes, pelting him with stones.
They beat him to his knees before Aurelius.
Through closing eye and bloody hair,
he still manages to smile.

That strange sound is Hengist laughing.

'Kill him', said Aurelius.
'Do it now and do it quickly,' adds Uther,

One strike of Adolf's sword,
the smiling head is in the dirt.

'We will bury him with honour,'
said Aurelius, eyeing Gorlois.
'In the heathen fashion,
with a mound of earth to cover him.
And pray no good comes to his soul.'

'He was a worthy foe, a famous fighter,'
said Uther, watching Gloucester,
waiting for objections that never came.[2]

The brothers walk among the dead.
An exasperated, blood washed Uther
beside his brother's polished finery.
The only blood on him is on his boots.

Even in defeat Hengist had out thought them.
He had chosen to stand and fight,
knowing he would lose, knowing

---

[2] The combat between Gloucester and Hengist and Aurelius' strange order to honour the latter by raising a mound over him in accordance with 'heathen practice' are in Laȝamon.

The Boys would bleed so many men
they could not continue north against his sons.

'Time for talking,' said Uther.
Aurelius, now king,
looks first to Merlin,
who nods, and so agrees.

2 The Punishments [3]
(*Gwydion remembers as he rides to Uther's court.*)

Math's ban went out
against our meat and drink.
We hungered
in the wastelands,

hunting, but knowing
we had no future,
finally went in.
Math, most eloquent of men,

gagging on rage and humiliation.
A glacier about to avalanche,
watching us approach
his ornate wooden throne.

Arglwyd, I said, dyd da it.
The formal greeting of the court,
braving his silence:
my brother ready to bolt.

You are here to repay me?
He carved each word
onto the air between us.
Lord, let your will be done.

If it had been my will, shaking,
there would not be
men dead, men maimed,
farms burnt, crops ruined.

---

[3] This is a version of part of *Math Uab Mathonwy*, edited by Ian Hughes for the Dublin Institute for Advanced Studies, (hereafter DIAS) 2013.

You cannot pay for the insults
you have done to me,
or atone for the death of Pryderi
or the harm you did the girl.

That wand. His hand,
no longer shaking, struck
with surety and speed
beyond my competence.

My twitching brother,
a trembling doe
too swiftly done
for disbelief.

Remembering an open window,
thinking peregrine or swift and
if I were quick then he was faster.
The faintest flick, an insect landing.

He touched me with that stick
and I an antlered stag,
baffled by walls, stone floors
so many humans.

His words were maggots in my skull:
You were equal partners in this crime
so now go forth together
with the nature of the form you wear,

and when their season comes
desire will drive you to each other
and though you know it to be wrong
you will mate, producing offspring.

Return with it, a year from now.

A year, no waking moment free
from fear. Alert, prepared to flee.
I saw the strongest stag run down
and shredded for a hunter

by his pack of slobbering hounds.
The wolf pack preying on us
cutting out the weakest
their death cries in my ears.

Fear understood along the nerves
in tensing muscles, panicked pause.
instinctive flight. And in the season,
the big stags fought for mating rights

but I was driven, even in the act
knowing this was my brother.
Hatred for Math, a constant ache
defiling the safest day.

Until, compelled we moved
towards the compound
braving the baying dogs
we could hear behind the walls.

Math came out to greet us.
Eagerly I waited for that wand.
He tricked us. Struck.
And I was sow; my brother boar.

Another year. Another mating.

Returning once again.
No longer wanting my revenge.
Wanting to be human,
to use the words

trapped behind my tongue.
Again he tricked us.
Wolves this time, predators,
thrilled to chase and kill.

But the gravitational pull
of the pack. Everything
with the pack, for the pack.
Nothing done that didn't help the pack.

A vague unease;
compassion's ghost
for the pigs we hunted,
the deer we tore apart.

With our cub,
back to the walls,
the baying dogs,
and Math.

I am content, he said.
I offer you my friendship
and forgiveness.
The final blow.

We were reborn human,
on our knees before him.
In our filth before his finery.
Take them to the hot baths.
See they are fed and groomed,
then lead them to my chamber.

Chapter One. Gwydion

This, my son, is how I met your father.

There was a man at home in the shadows.
His favoured place at the edge of the light
where ambiguity becomes magic.

Arriving after the great gate had been closed
and the guards were set for a winter's night.

The assistant, breathless, sought the Gate Keeper,
Grey Bold Mighty Grasp, who looked up from his food:
'Knife has gone to meat. The gates are shut.
Who is allowed to enter? Recite the rules.'

'The son of a lawful king,' the lad replied.
'Or a tradesman whose skills are needed at the court.'

'And which of those is he?'

'By appearance and speech, a nobleman.
By bearing one who walks at ease
amongst the great. His clothes
and weapons announce his wealth.'

'But who is he?' asked the Porter.
'What kind of man? What is his rank?
His trade? What is his family?
It is your job to ascertain these facts.'

His food was no cooler
before his assistant returned.

'He is the chief bard of the Island of Prydain,
the finest storyteller in the world
and the best of harpers, he says.

His name is Gwydion son of Don
and to prove it,
he will turn me into a mouse
if I don't open the gate.'

'There was a Gwydion son of Don,
who was chief bard before the Romans came.
Before the Druids even. A mighty magician
who made a ship from seaweed
and turned a bird into a boy.
Let him in. Cat's hungry.
Can't have him eating you, can we?
Uther's in a foul mood, and has been
since he returned from Ireland.
A story might gentle the blade.
We'll soon know if he's lying.
And God have mercy on him if he is.'

2

Gwydion the storyteller
steps into a version of himself.
The smoky hall lined with iron men,
bright, shiny, awkward,
dreaming a glorious future:
fame in battle, marriage,
their own estates and children.
Or rusting to the benches.
Bent, battle scratched,
stale veterans going sour
watching their time leaking away
like spilt ale down a long hill,
no longer believing in a future,
their chances fading like their hair.
Becoming the characters
they derided when they arrived:
too old to fight, too poor to fuck.

Don't patronise them.
We are born into stories we did not write.
Happy the men and women at home in theirs.

Uther Pendragon, at the high table,
surrounded by his court officials,
attendant lords, and a woman
with hair the colour of midnight in a cave
laughing with the man beside her.

Uther comes towards him,
with the shambling swagger
of a horseman after an epic ride,
shouldering his way through an imagined crowd.

He stops in front of Gwydion,
toe to toe, inspecting him.
'I need a bard. Heard you're good.
Had the last one thrown off the roof.'

He smiles, his head to one side,
'I like that. You didn't ask me why.
Because you know I'm going to tell you.
He told a story about the House of Brutus,
how The Thin Man had my father killed
then manipulated my brother's bodyguard
into killing him as well.'[4]

He turns towards the muttering faces.
They've all heard that story.
'Well that's utter bollocks init.'[5]
His hands throwing words across the room.
'A disgruntled servant knifed my dad.

---

[4] The Thin Man is Vortigern.
[5] Geoffrey, Wace and Laʒamon narrate the murder of Uther's father by a disgruntled servant. Pages or lines later, all three have Aurelius state, as a fact, that Vortigern murdered him.

I made enquiries.' Four syllables, loitering
unpleasantly. Something to be avoided.

'I fought with Huns. I mean with them
and against them. Allans, Goths, Lombards.
I know tribal warriors. These aren't Romans
who switch loyalties faster than you refill your cups.
It would take some kind of deviant Christ
to pull that miracle; to make
a tribesman turn on his ring giver.' [6]

He saunters back to Gwydion.
'My court needs a bard. Tell me three stories:
one now, here, for the drinkers at the benches;
one for my officers in my room;
one for my lady in her chamber.
Job's yours if they're good. If they ain't,
we'll throw you off the roof
for claiming to be someone you're not.'

The storyteller bows.

'But first, I'll tell you one.'

The drinkers at the benches settle.
The night loses its edge.
Pendragon, chief of warriors;
they admire, respect, adore
although he terrifies them all.[7]

---

[6] Throughout this book, Uther's knowledge of late Imperial history is 'uneven' by modern standards. He also seems to know some stray facts and sayings from earlier Greek and Persian times.

[7] Geoffrey of Monmouth seems to have misunderstood *Pendragon* and linked the name to a dragon banner made in imitation of a comet. It's more likely that Pendragon meant chief or first warrior. The story Uther tells is Geoffrey's explanation of how and why Stonehenge was built.

'My brother, the King of Britain,
by right of conquest and inheritance,
decided the British Lords
who'd died on Salisbury Plain
deserved a fitting monument.

So he holds a great council,
and everyone chips in.

Like all councils, no one can agree.

Merlin walks in. The fiend himself.
I'll get you a monument, he says.
It will stand for eternity.

Where is it, asks my brother.
In Ireland, says Merlin
and we all laughed at him.

Except the king, who sends me,
with an army, to get this Giant's Ring.
The locals pissed themselves
when they heard why we'd arrived.
They thought it was the best joke, ever.
So we taught them not to laugh at us
and finally arrived on this god-forsaken,
wind-raked hill in the middle of a great green nowhere.
There's stones. Huge, upright stones.
And we just stood and stared at them.

Try moving them, says Merlin.
We dug and pulled and pushed all day.
The stones stayed put.
Then Merlin mumbles some words
and did that thing with his hands,
like he's tying knots in the air.

Try now, he says, so to humour him,
we pushed a stone, and it fell over.
Stone turned to feather!
We hauled them to the coast,
watched by the astonished locals,
then sailed and dragged them
all the way to where you see them now.
A monument to British lords
slaughtered by Hengist and their own stupidity.
Now,' he says to Gwydion, 'top that.'

3

He will not try,
not knowing how Uther may react
to being beaten here, in this game.
They will not ask, why this story?
He can only throw the pebble in the pond.
He can't predict how far the ripples run.

'After The Great Slaughter,[8]
when the tribes were broken
and the Great Queen died in despair,
a prince was struggling home.

He'd lost his weapons,
retainers and horse.
Hadn't eaten for days.
He stumbled along the valleys,
staggering up and over the hills.
His life could only get worse.

---

[8] This story was suggested by Martin Carthy's singing of 'The Devil and the feathery wife'. I've changed everything except the terms of the deal and the wife's solution.

He knows the Romans will steal his cattle,
burn his farm, enslave his kin.
If he gets home, he can't stop them;
if they find him there, they'll kill him.
But he keeps on: beaten, not broken.'

Rumbling approval betrays their interest.
Been there; done that.

'It was a dark night, no moon, no stars,
and he's stumbling along through the trees
in the valley below Maen Llwyd.
At the point where the path forks,
he sees in front of him a darkness,
darker than darkness, and as he watches
it grows even darker, a shimmering shimmering,
and the Devil on horseback blocking his path.

Down on your luck warrior?
No luck left to be down on.
Well, says the Devil,
offering him bread from his bag,

I do deals on nights like this,
with desperate men like you.
I have nothing to bargain with says our man.
But my friend, says the devil, you do.

Seven good years without effort or pain,
safe from your enemy's eyes,
wife and children growing old
with the comforts that money can buy.

At the end of those years,
bring a beast from your farm,
if I name it, you serve me in hell,
if I can't, you won't be harmed,
and you'll have been richer as well.'

He pauses, to let them consider
if they'd take such an offer.
Even if the devil speaks English
how could he lose?

Seven years of pleasure
for an eternity in hell?
The muttering subsides.
They're waiting to see
what this warrior will choose.

'He'd seen the sacred groves in flames.
The druids and their people slaughtered,
the tribes broken on that red, Roman line.
How could Hell be any worse?

So he agreed. Home to his wife.
They watched the Roman army trooping past.
Seven years to the day, as the sun was setting,
he said goodbye to his daughters and sons.
What's ails you husband, have you gone mad?
She nagged him 'til he confessed what he'd done.

What an idiot's bet, but leave it to me,
the Devil's a man and men can be fooled.
Put your life in the hands of God and your wife
as every sane husband should do.

Bring me bird lime, as much as we've got
and the feathers we pulled from the birds.

Stripped naked, they smeared her with stickiness
'til she was covered from navel to head.
Then she tipped out the feathers all over the floor
and she rolled and she rolled 'til she'd covered herself.
Now lead me to your devil with a halter round my neck.

At the place where the path splits
the Devil was waiting,
a gloating darkness.
He looked at the beast:
a daughter of Eve
from her navel on down,
but the strangest of fowl
from her navel on up.

By my tail, he said, what a terrible sight!
What perverted mating produced such a bird?
I'll be damned if I know what it is.
Thank you. I'll take it to hell.

That wasn't our deal!

What I said, and I quote:
If I name it, you serve me in hell.
If I can't, *you* won't be harmed,
and *you'll* have been richer as well.

I didn't mention the beast.
Or your family. Or your farm.
She'll make a fine addition
to the freak shows of hell.

The halter was gone from his hand.

That sound on the breeze?
It's my favourite tune.
A Roman patrol,
with your daughters and sons.

Before he could scream,
take me instead,
he was alone on the road
with the flames of his farm
lighting the way home.'

After the silence that followed
Uther is calling his name.
'This ring is yours.
If the other two are as good
I will be honoured to have you as my bard.'

'My Lord is very generous.
It would be my honour to serve,
if, at the end of my service,
you will grant me one request.'

'As long as it is in my power,
does not diminish that power,
compromise my honour
or endanger my life or those near to me.
And that is my promise
in the hearing of these witnesses.'

He can only throw pebbles in the pond.

Chapter Two. Uther

Having recognised the subtle choreography
of a well-run court; intricate, efficient, affable,
Gwydion steps into Uther's room to find the dancers paused,
watching Uther lose an argument with a royal messenger.

'I'd rather listen to their stories
than fight them for their stones.
Why doesn't he send Cornwall?
He's got an army and a fleet.'

The walls of Uther's private rooms
are blank. A space for doing business.
Desks for the scribes, a table
covered in a map of Britain.
A tattered list of marching times
between the major centres.

A gathering of court officials,
selected officers, household staff.
The elite, by their clothes,
and their casual Latin.
A bishop with his secretaries.
Men who have studied rhetoric,
the traditional upbringing
for boys aimed by their parents
at the Imperial Bureaucracy.

At home with Ovid, Virgil, or Pelagius,[9]
debating transformation
or up to date theology.
They like their stories subtle,
will listen carefully, in silence,

---

[9] Pelagius was a British heretic. For details see 'The Scribe's Story' in *A Man of Heart*.

then tell the storyteller
what he failed to understand.

The Dark-Haired Woman
turns to watch him.

'The duke says he is otherwise engaged…'

'Doing what? Growing roses?'

'…with his fleet, on the south coast, searching for pirates…'

'He's chasing a few thieves.
That's more important than an invasion?'

The messenger waits.

'Tell my brother, the king…'

Does anyone else notice
he looks to the woman
for an almost
imperceptible response?

'…I shall, of course, obey a Royal Command.'

Before the messenger has left the room,
Uther's officers have their orders
and have gone about their business.

2

They will not ask, why this story?[10]
He can only throw the pebbles in the pond.

---

[10] This story is based on the third part of *Math Uab Mathonwy*. The deliberately erratic sympathies of my version are not in the original.

The lady watching him: hostility,
curiosity, both?

'Imagine,' he begins,
'the third curse of an outraged mother:
*You will never have a wife from any race
living at this time, upon this earth.*'

He pauses.
This is the leprous guest
who cannot be evicted or ignored:
to grow old without a wife,
without estates, without
the possibility of heirs.

'The boy's uncle, her brother,
had cheated her malice twice,
humiliating her with trickery and magic
but this time was defeated.

So he went to his uncle, a greater wizard.
Without a wife, without heirs,
the lands that he accumulates
will pass to strangers.
He will be a name in the wind,
fading. Here's what they did:

Taking the bloom of meadow sweet, broom and oak
they made a woman out of flowers.

Curve and flair and fall of perfect form.
Soft where she should be soft,
tight where she should be taut,
the most perfectly formed woman
ever seen by any man.

She surfaced, gasping, blinking the room.
Three figures in the mirror,
one with no covering on its skin.

Flowering from one face lined as an oak
a bush of grey hair. The other, slighter,
still and watchful, like a hawk hunting.
She watches as the naked body in the mirror
is stroked, manhandled, prodded, probed.

They have the smugness of men
who have side stepped a problem
and anticipate applause.
This one, says Oak Man.
Oh she's perfect, says the other.
Finally. He'll be delighted.

They leave her alone in the mirror.
The petals heaped in piles on the floor,
suggest failed human forms.

Maids bring clothes that itch her skin,
bright stones that weigh her down,
then lead her to another room.
Oak Face and Hawk and a third,
his beard like grass on a sand dune.
A fledging bird that hasn't learnt to fly.
Fluff on spindle legs, mouth open, demanding food.
She is left with Not Quite, shuffling and hesitant,
struck dumb and awkward by her presence.
Finally undressed he does what he does
and she doesn't understand, but by the time
he falls asleep it's obvious he likes his present.

He brings her gifts, trying to discover
what she likes, or wants,
understanding that she doesn't know.

Both orphans, both without a mother.
She is the ultimate amnesiac
with no childhood to forget.
Language without memory.
At the feast she stares at nothing,
intimidated by the ease the stupidest
master the rules that confound her.

A rougher man might bruise to violence.
Young, wanting to be liked, he
persists in his baffled kindness,
discovering a stranger he can only watch
from the wrong side of the river.

But a mother's curse is not so easily avoided.
 The young lord must attend the king,
perform his loyalty, hop for crumbs,
dropping from the royal table.'

(Careful, but they're nodding.)

'Her lord abandons her to visit Oak Man:
the annual rutting parody
when men migrate in herds to court
and grovel before power.

She sleeps in his absence.
Walks the circuits of the walls
looking out at a world she's hardly tasted.
In her damp stone rooms,
she sheds the scratchy cloth,
staring at the stranger in the mirror
who longs to walk naked in the sun.
Alone, drifting round the castle walls
late one evening she hears a hunt.
Knowing her lord and master husband
would offer the hunter hospitality,

sends a messenger. A prince no less.
The sight of her empties his mind.
He fumbles the normal courtesies.

The huntsman is astonishing.
The wave before it breaks.
He speaks words she doesn't hear;
small birds alighting on a tree
after a storm has rinsed the air bright.
The most exquisite song she's heard.
He is beautiful and clever.

They are swept into her bed,
where she discovers Not Quite's efforts
were a sad attempt to whistle bird song.
She discovers laughter. She craves him.
Branch and flower and leaf craving sunshine.

Lost in the specifics of first passion,
she cannot know they have become a cliché:
illicit lovers, doomed to disappointment,
and whatever punishment society approves.

In the morning he says,
Lady, I should leave you.
You will not she replies, and so he stays.
On the third day, he says, Lady,
the owner of this place will soon return.
As he dressed, they decide upon a plan.
There is only one way they can be together.
He gives her lessons in deceit.

When her lord returns, she seems upset.
He speaks to her: she won't reply.
What's wrong with you, he asks.
Are you not well? I was afraid my lord.

You were away. And I began to wonder
what would become of me if you did not return.

Dry your tears woman,
unless God reaches down
and strikes me from the clouds
I can't be killed. I told you that.

But I don't understand.

He had not dared believe she cared.
My uncle wrapped me
in such powerful magic,
no harm can touch me.

You told me there is only one way
you can be killed.
How is that possible?
Seduced by her concern,
he explains the details.

She sends word to her absent lover:
Make me a spear,
worked only on a Sunday,
when everyone's at mass.
Sharpen its point for a year.

The second annual absence. He returns.
My love, I'm just a foolish woman.
I was worrying again.
I can't imagine how you can be killed.
So to put her mind at rest,
he performs the absurdity.
One foot on the bath; one foot on the goat.
The canopy cracking above his head.
The lover hurls the spear.

But it doesn't kill him.
(Did he skip a Sunday?
Did they use the wrong animal?
Did the uncle leave something unsaid,
to insure the insurance?)
The wounded boy becomes a wounded bird
and stutters away into the hills.

He has polished his lust on a year of her absence,
scraping away at his spear.
But his imagination has drifted from memory
into the liminal theatre of desire
where the astonishing fact of her beauty
becomes a pornographic abstract
in the feral rut of his dreams.

The husband gone,
obligations contaminate their pleasure.
He must subdue his new kingdom.
Her kisses are a gentle rain that goes on far too long.
The exquisite bird song fades
between the silence and the monosyllables.
He wants to moan about their tenants.
She wants to offer him advice.
It's a relief to hear the uncle
has found the wounded husband.

He has his excuse to leave.
She sheds her clothes
and walks into the hills,
with maids, for modesty.

First the uncle must find the damaged bird,
sing it down from its branch,
then nurse it back to human health,
human bitterness, human hatred.
With the king's permission

they can hunt the lovers.
Self-righteous, vindicative, persistent.
How to outrun a man who has been a wolf,
or hide from one who was a bird?
The girl is walking in the hills,
when they catch her near a lake.

They drown her terrified maids.

Grey rocks, grey lake, grey clouds
and she a golden singularity
in a desert landscape,
nudged by the breeze.
Despite their violence,
she stands her ground;
naked, unembarrassed, unafraid.
Her voice soft as the failing light:

You designed the world's desire,
then gave it to this child,
as sex toy, brood mare, serving maid.
Why give me language and intelligence
and then demand that I be silent and obey?
You made me human, with free will,
but then denied my right to choose.
 You expect me to be grateful?
How many lives have you abused,
to demonstrate your competence.
This knot you made but can't undo.

Blame me, then strike and walk away.

They do not bargain.
She has no male kin to pay her fine.
There is no compensation
she can offer for the shame
inflicted on her husband.

Transformed into an owl,
she will shun the light
and endure the eternal hatred
of all the other birds.

The lover, trapped,
sends messengers.
You made her perfect.
How could I not be dazzled?

Man to man, what will the boy accept
as compensation for his injury and shame.

I will give you all my lands.
My castles. My treasury.

Stand where I stood, says the boy.
I'll stand where you did
and throw a spear at you.
He agrees, but because
the woman made me do it,
let me place a stone between us.

Fair's fair. The mighty spear
goes straight through stone
and him.' The audience cheers.
The bishop signals. The talking stops.
'The implications of your story.
An unrepentant Eve, blaming God…'

Uther interrupts. 'Your story fades.'

Gwydion bows, 'My Lord is very kind.
I am flattered that you say so.'

Uther, surprised, speechless, but amused.

'My task is not to tell my listeners what to think,
but to give them things to think about.
Stories with neat endings shut down conversations.'

Chapter Three. Ness

The queen safe in her chambers
protected by her husband's walls
guarded by his watchful men.

In a winding stair
a door in a blank wall.
Splintered wood,
undressed stone.
The watchful guard
nodding welcome.
Knock and enter.

Maidmutter flamecrackle.
On the stairs, feetpadding
cloak drag pike chink.
Rushes on the floor.
Beneath the window
muffled wind dragged
courtyard voices.
Desire and common sense
arguing the toss.
A trunk. A bed,
a chair beside the fire,
a stool. An anchorite's austerity
but for the full-length mirror.

The lady's chamber,
usually full of wives
of prominent men,
their maids, their daughters.

Only two blonde serving girls
in the window seat,
dozing at their sewing.

Sitting on a low stool,
poking the fire with a stick,
she is wearing a plain wool dress,
over a simple white shift.
Her skin like mother of pearl,
hair black as the raven,
lips like spilt blood.

She has hitched her skirts above her knees
and the curve from ankle to shadow
is the finest line he's ever seen.

The songs do justice to her looks.
But she is not a princess.

The Saxons would call her:
'Ness, the Lord's gebedda.'[11]
Rumour at the court claims
he hasn't touched another woman
since she first shared his bed.
Witchcraft mutter the jealous wives,
black magic the lusting husbands.
Another rumour, far more scandalous:
she has civilised the beast
and taught him how to rule.

'Your story was a mess.
Sympathy for the girl.
Approval of the men.
You can't have both.

Your magicians made a grave mistake.
Like any father who makes a girl
then trades her off to please another man

---

[11] Literally his bed sharer. Not a derogatory term in a world where it took some courage to close your eyes when another person was present.

in the male game of bloodlines,
Mi a'th roddais i ŵr.[12]
No one asked her what she wanted.
You played god, and like your god
gave your creation the ability to choose
then punished her for using it.

Sit down. Tell me,
why did you leave out half the story?'

Ambushed by hostility.
Mouth moving
to cover his surprise:

'If a story needs an audience,
not all audiences deserve the story.'

Leaving him to his discomfort,
she feeds the fire, then continues:

'There's another woman.[13]
Because this one's in a story
she is young and beautiful
and there's a boy
lust is eating from the inside out.
He takes her memory to bed.
A glimpse, the fragment
of a sentence overheard,
the way she turns her head.
And his dream mistress
flowers in the space
between waking and sleep.

---

[12] A legal formula: 'I have given you to a man.' With all the power imbalance the grammar implies. *The Welsh Law of Women,* edited by Owen and Jenkins, University of Wales press, 2017.

[13] Ness is telling him a version of the first part of *Math uab Mathonwy.*

His brother is a powerful magician
and he sees the boy is shrivelling.
Won't eat, won't speak, won't play
and when he blurts out his confession,
he doesn't say, in your dreams, child,
she doesn't love you, not a little, not at all,[14]
learn to live with disappointment.
He says: Minheu a baraf.[15]

He's the famous go to Mr. Fixit.
He must prove competence,
not think of consequence.

To get the girl alone,
they have to start a war.
He tricks a southern prince:
steals his pigs. He offers
horses, bridles, saddles,
golden shields and coin
till greed overwhelms
the prince's common sense
and when he wakes,
to find his horses, bridles
saddles, golden shields
are rotting mushrooms
he musters his kingdom.
So indeed there was a war.
Men died. The prince died.
But the brothers crept back into the court
and raped the girl.

When the king finds out,
he's furious. Deceit, betrayal,
from within his own family.

---

[14] This line is Luned's sensible words to Owein. From *Owein*, edited R.L. Thompson, DIAS, 1986.

[15] It is I who will organise this.

He can't bring back the prince,
or the men who died,
or restore the maimed.
But he does the right thing by the girl,
then calls the brothers.
You have acted like beasts
though you look like men.
I shall make you animals.[16]

But still he didn't learn.
It should be a triad:
Three women destroyed by Gwydion Fix-it.
Three women and not once,
not once does he ask one of them
what she wants,
or even consider that what she wants
might be important.
All that matters is he prove his skill.
Nothing beyond Minhau a baraf.

The world reduced to predator and prey.
Everyone comes to conquer,
no one wants to trade.'

In the silence after the prosecutor
has presented her evidence
he looks less like a man in the dock,
than a hawk on its perch
blinking at the fire, undecided:
flee, stay, strike.

She hasn't raised her voice.

Between indignation and shame,
why, of all the words he could have used:

---

[16] *The Punishments* describes what happened next.

'You know the story well, lady,
but your resentment sounds personal.'

Or why she smiled.

'As well as you do.

While he plans this war,
Uther will ask you
to entertain me.
Come back tomorrow,
I might tell you why.

Now I must be at my lord's pleasure.'

She smiles at the ambiguity.

'These girls will keep you warm.'

He bows. 'Only if that's their wish.'
Which surprises all four of them.

2

The same room,
she's reading by the fire.
Maids at the window seat,
looking up from their sewing,
smiling as he enters.

They had been surprised.
His greed for information,
his curiosity about their lives.
The ease he speaks their language.

A tragedy in a better world
where such things rarely happened,
their stories were clichés
in a world where men are killed
and women used and sold.

Slavers burnt their homes,
killed the fighting men, the elderly,
the over young. The fittest led away.
The girls and women used.
Or sold. Two pretty blonde girls,
cheap as a job lot at an auction,
bought by Uther, gifted to Ness
who they worship as a substitute divinity.

He knows they have told her everything.

He has made two more friends
opening negotiations for a third.

'My father was bard teleu
to a kindly prince whose kingdom
could be crossed by a lazy toddler
in a single sleepy afternoon.
When the prince was murdered by his cousin
my father retired to his estate.'

She adds more sticks to the fire.

'One night there was a storm,
and at our gate, a lord,
out hunting, seeking shelter.
Not demanding; asking.

My father was not rich,
but he fed his royal guest
while I waited on them:

we had few servants.
He insisted that I sit with him.
He was funny, charming,
I'd never met anyone like him;
interesting but interested.
He made me laugh.
I went to bed, amused.
I'd waited on the brother of a king.
Then my door was pushed open.

I went from virgin daughter to royal whore
in the time it took him to cross my chamber
and throw my bedclothes on the floor.
He said if all the women in the world
were his to choose, I was the one he'd pick.'

She stirs the fire.

How much is wishful thinking?
Too stunned to be terrified
by his invasion of her chamber.
The place where she had played with dolls.
Like a great wave, collapsing,
the bewildering shock; her baffled outrage,
his greedy persistence at her body.

Her mind had left. Perhaps next morning
while he was busy, hands and lips and tongue,
she knew she had to talk,
make him see more than a tasty bit of flesh,
terrified of what would happen when he left.
Or perhaps that was retrospective.
Perhaps she'd just blurted words.
Something he said about Aurelius,
had angered her: Sounds
as though he wants the title,
not the job, and he'd gone silent.
Weeks later he'd explained.

I'd never thought of him like that.
If I were king, I'd do what I must do,
to the best of my ability
regardless of the personal cost.
But you were right.
He wants proud men on their knees,
soliciting his good opinion. And me,
I want the job. I don't want
blisters on my arse from sitting
on the throne, while well-dressed men
line up to tell me what they think
I want to hear them say. I want
to unify the province, defeat its enemies
bring the predictability of peace
to every man woman and child in the island.
And the difficulty of that
excites me just as much as you do.

'On the third day we left
with only the clothes that I was wearing.
Embarrassed to meet my father,
until I learnt that Uther had his blessing
before he stormed my room.

My father was well paid.
A title, an estate, some bright hard shiny things.
He sold me like a carcass at the market
and before I left he gave me a white rod
so he wouldn't have to pay
for anymore 'transgressions' in the future.[17]

I thought Uther was going to kill him.

---

[17] My anachronism. In later Welsh law, the father of an unmarried girl had to pay a fine if she had intercourse. The white wand was the sign of a prostitute. A father who gave it to his daughter was publicly accepting and announcing her promiscuity, so he was exempt from future fines. In this case his actions would be unjustified.

An item in the royal baggage.
The servants trying to imagine me
without my clothes.
Then he'd ride back,
take me off the road,
against a tree, on my knees,
flat on my back in the grass.
Shameless as rutting beasts.
He left nothing for them to imagine.

And now he's off again
leaving me in charge.'

'There's trouble in the north, lady.
Not just the Irish.
Hengist's sons are restless.'

'The bishops call them,
The Instruments of God's wrath,
punishing the sinful Britons.'

'The peace won't hold.
If nothing else,
they have a father to avenge.'

'I never heard from mine again.'

In the mirror she still sees
the body Uther can't resist,
but forming in its shadow,
in the corners of the mirror's room,
Aestrild's rotting corpse
still fretting at the knots
that bind her to her daughter.[18]

---

[18] Aestrild's story is told in *A Presentment of Englishry*. After Locrin abandons Gwendolin for her, Gwendolin raises an army, kills Locrin, and then has Aestrild and her daughter condemned for witchcraft and tied together and thrown into the Severn.

Chapter Four. Ygrayne

What is it about beauty,
about a body's shape,
that disturbs thought?
Unwanted turbulence
to undermine the castle walls
and infiltrate the keep?
When the mind recoils,
the body still leans in.

'Storyteller!' Uther,
in the bustle of the court
as it prepared for his departure.
Obviously amused,
he took Gwydion by the arm,
and steered him to a corner.

'Or should we call you Varus?
You walked right into it, didn't you?
You may be the best of storytellers
but you're a poor judge of character
if you underestimate my woman.

The Irish want their rocks back.
Aurelius is sick
so I must go with Merlin
to offer them as much land
as their corpses will require.

I can't afford to have Gorlois
tossing a coin to decide if
he'll come when he's called.
His victory celebrations
will require a storyteller.
Go to Cornwall. Sound him out.
See if he'll work with us.

You should be safe.
You are now a Royal Bard.
Ness will claim her story
next time you meet.'

2

The mind is a flexible thing,
otherwise even Gwydion, shapeshifter,
would have doubted his.
The weather had broken as he travelled west.
The rain, blurring vision as he turned off the road,
stopped abruptly as he crested a hill, astonished
by the imperial past mapped out below him
in the squared geometry of a villa complex.

A dressed stone wall, a gate, armed men.
His escort and their horses lead away,
a court official came to be his guide
through the labyrinthine gardens, between
whitewashed walls, below red tiled roofs,
running rivers that crashed onto the path
beside the battered, swaying roses.
Babbling some kind of Brito-Latin,
the chamberlain gentled him down corridors,
where the shaky lights of oil lamps
made the building insubstantial.
A bath house, warm water, sweet-scented oils,
a bedroom, where the hypocaust was working.
The longest wall, crudely whitewashed,
fading to show, as ghostly stains, four human figures.

In the dining room, the mosaic had been repaired
by someone with less skill than dedication.
Beneath the central Chi Ro symbol,
the face had been replaced by different coloured tiles.

A headless figure perched on a bent horse,
was hunting a confused beast. Or perhaps
the bent spear was a leash and he was taking it for a walk.

In the villa of Gorlois Duke of Cornwall,
everyone looking over his shoulder
waiting for the whip to crack.

3

Gorlois has destroyed a pirate base.
Burnt three ships, captured two.
He'd crucified their crews along the coast.
A celebration needs a storyteller.
The Duke of Gloucester will be there,
and Ygrayne, Cornwall's wife,
will grace the evening
with her bejewelled presence.
He is to entertain her
while the serious men
talk serious men's business.

In front of her mirror,
maids fussing with her finery
preparing her for the feast,
when Gwydion enters.

Is this what Paris saw
watching Helen
prepare herself for Menelaus?

That she is beautiful,
no one would deny,
but she's no ornament.
He knows a witch
when he sees one,
frightened into cruelty.

She is as beautiful
as snow-capped Yr Wyddfa
gilded at sunset
because distance hides
ice and rock
and the bitter wind
that freezes any pilgrim.

Her predecessor, married at twelve,
to guarantee the loyalty of her father
and unify the western tribes;
no child playing with her toys
but trained from birth to be a chieftain's wife,
baffled by a husband who demanded
(outside the bedroom) she be silent and ornate.
When her father was assassinated
and his place taken by no relative of hers
Gorlois had disposed of her and married this one.

No one knows where she came from.
They say she's of the fairy folk,
blown in on the wind,
washed up on the strand,
though he can't imagine her
surprised and shipwrecked on the beach.

She would have glided over the wave tops
unruffled by the tempest, using
her drowning companions as stepping stones.
Rumour says Ireland, or the Western Isles,
but where family is defining,
she's no one's daughter. No one at court
remembers when she first arrived,
nor how. She might have been a slave.
But she had captivated Gorlois
and that prim, moral man,
was soon creeping to her bed at night
while his wife was sleeping solitary in his.

Rumour has noticed the way she's making friends
amongst the local chieftains.
For which lord doesn't have a lady
by whichever name he calls her
and what lady doesn't have at least one maid
who has a sister or a mother,
who has a friend, or a friend
with an aunt or a niece,
and a message can be sent
or taken on a visit,
woven into a stream of harmless gossip.
A sisterhood of devoted spies
who sit in window seats, invisibly sewing,
who loiter at the table with the wine,
who spend the night with a man
who might say something
his hangover will erase come morning.

But which storyteller worth the name
is not the instant friend of stable boy,
cook, door keeper, cup bearer,
bath attendant, serving maid and kitchen wench?

The servants fear Gorlois,
who fears his wife's unfaithful.
(The servants swear she's not.
They say her promise is gold in hand.)
But no male dares return her smile,
share a joke, or loiter in her company,
unless he wants to decorate
the dung heap with his corpse.
They look away, and hurry past
because a smile is not worth dying for.

She knows one truth: everyone
who meets her craves her notice.
They want her to approve,

applaud, admire. They want her
to like them. She doesn't need sex,
or bribery. It's as natural as wanting
to be warm during the winter, or dry
after a storm. So she turns her smile at Gwydion
and though it can make the dead
get up and crawl towards her,
though it draws the fluttering lamp flame
and the walls edge closer
this man does not care for her approval.

Rumour says that when the women he encounters,
wives of patrons, bored with husbands who ignore them,
signal he'd be welcome in their beds,
he has learned to turn them down
and still retain their loyalty and affection.

Fathers and husbands trust him
with their daughters, sisters, wives.
They'll leave him in the ladies' chambers
to entertain them while the men get drunk.

That rare thing: an interesting man.

4

'They say that I'm the fairest of them all.
What does that mean?'

Gwydion tries to settle by the fire.
He does not want to be her enemy.[19]

'The fairest of them all?

---

[19] The story that follows is based on *Breudwyt Maxen Wledic*, edited by Brynley F. Roberts for DIAS, 2005.

In the days when Vortigern still ruled,
13 men dressed as imperial messengers
tattered, scruffy, boldly diffident,
as though they had slept for half a century
and hadn't heard the Empire was defunct.

The Emperor sent us, one began,
to find the most beautiful woman in the world,
in the most beautiful of castles
on the banks of the most beautiful river.
The Emperor saw this in his dream.

And everywhere we went,
said number two,
the people pointed to their local fort
as though a bank and ditch
a crumbling fence, a rotting gate
excelled the Theodosian Walls.
All the local girls without the marks
of plague or pox. This man swore
it was his daughter, that man
swore it was his brother's wife.
Some even claimed it was their mother
once upon a time.

Not one looked more lovely than the next,
by a muddy stream that dried up every summer,
or a stinking tidal mud flat the local poet praised.
And so we wandered for a year, knowing
we could not go home without an answer,
knowing there could be no answer.

It is a fool's errand,
said number three.

We cannot call
the Emperor a fool.

We have seen how
he reacts to failure.

But it is our shoe leather
worn out with walking
our horses dying
of exhaustion.

Vortigern interrupts:
And if she were an imbecile,
or a well-known sadist?

And then, said five, we stood upon a mountain
everything exactly as our master had described.
And at the end of the river, in a town on the coast,
in a room full of gold, on a chair made of ivory…'

He is white noise in the room.
She is staring at herself
in the polished bronze of the mirror.

'The most beautiful woman in the world.
We went down on our knees.
Our master sent us to you, we said.
Come with us and he
will make you Empress of the World.

She smiled at us and none of us
will ever be the same again.
Look around, she said, in a voice like a kiss.
What do I lack? I don't need a husband…'

That small sound of mirth that is not laughter.

'Another began, No, no, remember,
we wandered off the path towards woodsmoke
and saw the most beautiful woman in the world

stirring a pot of soup. Come with us, we said,
the Emperor of the World wants to marry you.
She stared at us, then laughed and went on stirring.'

Now she is laughing.

'No, said another…

                    There are thirteen of you,
interrupted Vortigern.
Have you ever agreed on anything?

Their embarrassed silence admitted they had not.

When Helen was the world's desire,
the Greek lords all agreed their gods
had made the perfect female form.
Perhaps the world was different then.
Perhaps it's just a story. If thirteen tired,
and desperate men cannot agree,
how could those warring Greeks?

Vortigern saw they had no desire
to understand what he had said.
You are welcome here, rest awhile.
You have travelled far and seen much.

I am eager to hear your stories.

We cannot stay, one said. We have heard
there is a greater fortress further north,
home to the last legion. And there, perhaps
we'll find the woman of our master's dream.

He gave them guides to the turf wall.

Perhaps they're trekking still
having crossed the grey sea.
The survivors sledging onwards
hauling their tattered possessions
into the endless darkness,
of snow, ice, howling winds
death and disappointment.'

The maids have finished.
She turns, black hair scattered with gold.
She is as beautiful as a painless death.

'Can't you give a direct answer to my question?'

'It means you won't starve any time soon.'

Before he can regret his irritation,
her unexpected smile
cut the ground from under him.

Watching him in the mirror,
she sang:

'The emperor had a wife,
he told her of his dream,
So she sent her men
to follow his thirteen.

She gave them strictest orders,
if this woman's ever seen;
kill them, bury her.
There can only be one queen.'

They are both laughing when the door opens.

5

Enter Gorlois. A trim man, a tidy man,
shrivelled to an habitual impatience.

His gravitas is wounded by their laughter.
His suspicions activated by her smile.
'Leave us,' he orders. 'Wait in the hall.'
Gwydion rises before he understands
the man is speaking to his wife.

Polite nothings about the estate,
about the quality of the food
served on imported African table ware.
The joys of hot water.

'Once this was normal,
in the days of Ambrosius,
when this was Ynys y Kedeirn.[20]
The whole province orderly.
Every man and woman
knowing their place.

Hengist is dead.
I see no evidence of roaming war bands,
no signs of immanent social collapse.
I see laziness and bad management
looking for excuses.
The House of Constantine
exaggerate the Saxon threat
so they can cling to power.'[21]

Nostalgia is a perverse mistress.
Memory's destructive sister,

---

[20] The Island of the Mighty.
[21] Uther claims descent from Brutus, but Gorlois is asserting his pedigree goes no further back than his father, who Gorlois insists usurped the throne.

compelled to tell her lovers
only what they want to hear.

'If Uther becomes king,
you share the same ambition:
a united province. Peace and order.'

'He ignores the elites who ruled
by right of birth and education.'

'Who were notoriously corrupt and incompetent.'

'Families older than Rome,
will be discarded or erased,
replaced by limb hackers
like this Urien who can't sign his name.
Without respect for tradition
there is no civilization.'

Unless the tradition's worthy of respect
there is nothing worth preserving.
This myth of perfect order, like all nostalgia,
perverts the present and cripples the future.

'For a man who claims he had no education,
Uther is an expert on the Empire.
He knows he'll need experienced administrators.'

'The finest military mind of his generation?
With no trained army to execute his plans.'

And round and round they go
till Gorlois tires of polite nothings.

'Why should I serve him?
The Rightful King of Britannia?
He's the son of a fool

who had as much right to this island as my dog.
You don't think I could defeat him?'

'This is a man who understands violence.
War has been his nursery, classroom, and playground.
He would rather go to a massacre than attend a feast.
Rather rest amongst the slain than sleep in a bed.'

'I've heard he'd rather screw his concubine
than do a full day's work.'

'Can you beat him? No.
Even if you had the skill,
your tribal army is mere landfill.
What will you do, squat in your hill forts,
pray for rain and hope his army rusts?'

'You are no longer welcome here.
Go now, before I forget myself.'

She is pacing the corridor.

Gwydion bows as he passes.
She does not have to ask.

6

Messengers met him at the Tamar.
Aurelius was dead. Poisoned.

Outnumbered ten to one,
Uther had triumphed in the west.
One hundred ships ferried the raiders to Britain;
only ten were needed to take survivors home.

Uther was heading to London to be crowned.
As they rode east, hurrying to meet him,

the landscape darkened around them:
a burnt settlement; an abandoned town,
its wall unfinished, its roofs broken.
Furtive survivors and timid ghosts
flitting at the edge of vision
scurrying away to share the shadows
with the rats. The starving dogs,
tottering between the fallen tiles,
no longer had the energy to bark.

In the fields a lost horse, a solitary cow.

Him? Or that play of intelligence and humour,
minus the hostility, like light on water?

Gwydion considered Gorlois
as though he were a character in a story
and his motivations could be analysed.
(Reminding himself that only martyrs and lunatics
are perfectly consistent.)

Despite the obvious signs
he was consorting with the heretics
no principle drove him. He hated Uther.
He hated himself for doing nothing
while the man who made him was destroyed.
Neither indecisive nor afraid,
he feared he was an indecisive coward.

As they continued east,
he realised the riders
were mapping the roads.

Nights beside a fire, with guards posted.
The stars above and memories.

'When you tell a story,' said Taliesin,
(The shining youth with the impish grin,
drinking Gwydion's mead during one of their many,
inevitable, enjoyable, discussions of their craft.)

'you tidy the world. Those men
who stagger through their lives
rushing from one disaster to another
can be credited with qualities
none of them possess.
Actions that result from fear,
resentment, personal animosity,
a headache or a troubled gut,
retrospectively become 'policy'
in the tidiness of your stories.'

'And your songs don't tidy the world?
Praise their courage preying on the weakest.
Praise their liberality with their stolen goods.
Call them kings and dignify the riders in the corn?
Your patrons act as though the seven deadly sins
were a check list for success.'

'Not sloth, sloth gets them killed.'

'You make an honest poem about your benefactors,
I'll compose a story without princes, kings, or magic.'

With Gorlois as the central character? Too static?
A painting on a wall or a figure in a tapestry,
to be unravelled and erased.

Chapter Five. First Crown Wearing

1 Power as Theatrical Performance

After Uther was crowned,
a man so at one with a horse
he'd make a Hun jealous,
he looked unsteady on a chair
like a man in a small boat,
rocked by a vicious cross-current.

A court official is reading a list.
Here is a man who loves numbers.
Who wants the world tidy as a calculation.
Using legal euphemisms:
default, distrain, deficit,
to prevent human misery
contaminating his balance sheet.

A list of tenants on the royal estates,
who have defaulted on their rent.
'We will distrain, with force if necessary.'
Uther is down from the throne, across the space,
before the terrified man can drop to his knees.

'I was hungry so you made me starve?
I was homeless so you burnt my shelter?

Share the seed in the royal granaries,
freely, with every farmer who defaulted.
 Tell them, Uther, their king, says,
their taxes are remitted for this year.
Next year we will reassess what they can pay.

Do you know what the Persians did to Crassus?[22]

---

[22] The Persians poured molten gold down his throat to mock his greed. Whether he was alive or dead before they started depends on the version you read.

Good. If I hear you've lined your purse,
I will do the same, first to your family,
while they're still alive, and after
you've had a week to think about it, then
I'll do the same to you. Do you understand?'

2

'…wouldn't have to do it twice.'

Uther, watching the maids undressing Ness.

'I had a tutor. A priest.
Before they killed him
he taught me that little bit of Bible.
I'm fairly sure it doesn't read:

I was naked and you raped me
I was hungry and you burnt my crops.

The empire was a cesspit of dishonesty.
I never met an Imperial official
who wasn't incompetent or on the make.'

While the maids remove her finery,
they talk, knowing whatever he says
will be carried into the court.
The maids have his permission.
They are free to babble in the kitchen.
The elder's mimicry of Uther,
hands moving, endlessly explaining,
is a favourite with the cooks.

'True, a frightened man is rarely loyal,
but a starving man's only got two choices.
When the Goths first crossed the Danube

Valens let them in but then his governor
thought he'd do them over. He starved them
until they were forced to sell their children;
one dog carcass for a child and that worked really well.
At Adrianople those same Franks
slaughtered an entire Imperial army.
20,000 soldiers dead in one hot dusty day.
The Emperor killed, hiding in an outhouse.'

'20,000 dead. So many grieving families.'

'Piss poor intelligence did for Valens.
He thought there were only 10,000 Franks.
Imagine the look on his face
when he marched into five times that number.'

She watches him in the mirror,
as the maids unbraid her hair.
There are versions of Uther;
violent, terrifying, brutal.
He can out ride, out drink, out fight
any of his retainers. His lack of fear
inspires his soldiers. But her Uther,
the one she sleeps beside,
slips out of his role as king.
A man not brutalised by circumstance?
Or another performance for an audience of one?
All these versions willing and able
to talk the hind legs off a donkey.

3 Pillow talk

Alone together.
Sex as the physical expression of mutual affection.

He tells her about the recent oath taking.
The lords pledge allegiance to their new king.

They go down on their knees,
place their hands in his, and swear
that they will be his loyal men.
The line forms, then disintegrates.

Uther stands and waits
until the last embarrassed pair
realise everyone is watching them
fighting over who goes next.

'It is a capital offence to start an affray
in the presence of the king.'

(How still, how silent the hall becomes.)

'But today we celebrate a new beginning.

My lords, it is so very simple.

Hengist landed three ships.
Less than two hundred men
unpicked this province,
at the same time Aetius
was mustering five hundred thousand
to fight Attila.'

More muttering.
What's that to them?

'If we work together for a common cause:
a united province run to the rule of law,
then nothing short of Caesar's thirty thousand
can trouble us. But

every time you fight amongst yourselves
you guarantee a thug with fifty men
is potentially a military catastrophe.

When the Saxons field a thousand,
you are history. Unless this bickering stops,
the privileges you're so desperate to retain,
the tribal heritage you eagerly proclaim,
will be swept into the past
and your corpses, and your children's corpses,
will fertilise someone else's crops.'

Now, he admits to Ness:
'I sounded like a dull tutor
lecturing a dim class.
I sat down: they began again.
I had the loudest executed.
Their lands are forfeit.
All males in their family will die,
the rest will be enslaved.
I have demanded hostages.
My horses are more rational.'[23]

4

The maids in splendour, their mistresses
hung with jewels, the smell of fragrances
invoking trade routes, men staggering
across deserts, to ports, where sailors
risked the crossing to bring small phials
of scented oils so these women
could be their lord's extravagance.

Gwydion recoils. Both women turn towards him.
Strange doubling. Like sisters, black haired
pale skinned, red lipped. A golden headband
studded with garnets and rubies on one,
the other wears her hair in Roman fashion,

---

[23] In Laȝamon the fight over precedence occurs at Arthur's court. I've muted his retaliation.

piled high and scattered with small jewels.
A Ness he's never met, hard and competitive,
impatient with her maids, shines in the light,
knowing Uther could have hired an army
with the stones she's wearing.

He retreats towards the corridor.
'Come in,' she says, 'come in, and shut that door.'
If staring is mandatory it brings no pleasure.
The prisoner invited to admire the instruments of torture
before the screaming starts.

He has no idea what these women talk about
when there's no men to overhear.
Later, he will ask Ness, and she will smile
and poke the fire and change the subject.

'Tell me,' says Ygrayne,
pleased to see a familiar face,
remembering shared laughter,
'this Merlin, this boy who scares hard men.
I'd heard Aurelius relied on him,
and every palm reader and stargazer,
alchemist, witch and potion peddler
clustered around, while the courtiers,
unsettled, unsure, afraid,
bought whatever magic was for sale.'

Gwydion says nothing.
It's easy to be a Merlin.
Evil has its own exquisite beauty,
shame and fear its aphrodisiacs.
Ness: 'I've never met him.
He's not invited to the feast.'

They are both staring at him.
His silence is no longer bearable.

But in the distance he can hear
the sudden grinding tear
as Fortune starts to turn her wheel.

5 The first crown wearing

Enter Gorlois. He has left his arrival
as late as possible to make a point.
He is self-contained. He is blank.
An automaton. His wife beside him,
as they walk the long aisle to the throne.
They are polite, in the brittle way
of people trying not to scream.
They are walking on ice,
knowing it must crack.
Holding their breath.

The court holds its breath.
There is no secret animosity here.
But Uther pays his debts.

She is alarming. All the women
stare in envy. She is wearing
a fortune in jewels. Her dress
is finest silk, and it hugs
the curve and flair of her.

Uther notes all this, without interest,
and turns his attention to Gorlois.
He offers him land, a principality
on the north side of the Severn.
Gorlois makes no attempt to hide his disappointment;
such paltry rewards for his great service.
If there is a dividing line between honesty and insult
no one has ever shown it to him.

6

Gwydion begins [24]

'A prince went hunting early in the day.
Blinked and the trees were all the same.
The paths fading amongst leaf litter.

Separated from his huntsmen,
he heard the earth
crushed by his horse's hooves,
heard the thick leaves
shift in the breeze,
heard the sound of his hounds and followed
until a clearing surprised him,
and in the clearing
a panicked stag, staggering and stupid
with fear and exhaustion,
and chasing it, a pack. Not his pack.
The whitest of white dogs
with the reddest of red ears,
and eyes like bottomless wells.

You'd think he'd know something was wrong,
but not Pwyll, Prince Act First And Then Repent At Leisure.
The white dogs killed the stag but he drove them off
and fed his own dogs on the steaming corpse.'

He pauses. Yes.
They know the etiquette.
This prince has crossed a line.

'Pwyll looked up from the ruined beast.

---

[24] This story is a version of *Pwyll Pendeuic Dyfed*, edited by R.L. Thompson for DIAS, 1957. Translating Annwfn as 'hell' is a gross oversimplification for the purpose of my story. The end owes something to Thompson's edition of *Owein*, DIAS, 1986.

The fern's curve gilded by sunlight
striking through the trees,
pillars of light confused by clouds of midges,
flies homing in on the gutted stag.

A dappled grey horse, huge,
its rider dressed for the hunt,
in fawn-coloured clothes,
horn slung around his neck,
watching him from the trees.
A bent note in the rustle of the forest.

Lord, says Pwyll, good day to you.
Though he shimmers like a reflection
disturbed on clear water.

I know who you are.
A voice too close to bird song;
incongruous for a huntsman.
And I do not greet you.'

He can read the audience reaction.
They understand this. Insult. Reparation.

'Is it your rank that prevents you, Lord?

God knows, It is not my rank,
it is your rank discourtesy.

What discourtesy do you see in me, Chieftain?

I have never seen a more grave discourtesy
and unless you compensate me appropriately,
I will carry your shame to the limits of your reputation.

Chieftain, if I have offended you,
I will gladly buy your favour.
But I do not know your rank.

I am a crowned king in my country.

What country is that, Chieftain?

Hell, says the other. I am Arawn,
King of Annwfn.

This is what you will do, says the stranger.
We will swop places for a year and a day.
You will be me, in my kingdom. You will have hunting,
feasting, carousing, poetry and music.
I will give you the finest woman in the world,
my wife, to sleep with every night.
Even she, and my most trusted chamberlains,
will not see through the deception.

But Chieftain, what will happen to my lands?

Minheu a baraf. At the end of the year
you will be called to a duel at a ford.
The man is trying to take my kingdom.
In your first pass you will wound him.
He will beg you to finish him off.
No matter his suffering, ignore him.
Strike one blow and no more.
If you strike him again,
he will recover and return. Now.
I will take you to hell.

When he arrived servants came to meet him.
He was undressed and after he had washed,
given fine silk robes. Then the horn was blowing,
calling them to the feast. He had not seen
a finer hall, the interior decked with gold.
He spent that first day in feasting and carousing.
He had never heard such poetry, or music,
the most beautiful woman he'd ever seen

sat beside him, and her talk was a wonder,
until the time came for them to sleep,
and he followed her to his bedroom.'

And now the first swerve.
Because what they want
is who put what, where, how often.

'He watched while she undressed.
He had never seen a more attractive body
or a face that smiled with such affection.
If God had reached into his head
found his ideal woman and made her real,
she would be Arawn's naked wife.

The prince lay at the edge of the bed,
turned his face to the wall,
and did not turn or speak until the morning.

Maybe this was hell, shot through with rainbows
or another paradise complete with snakes.
Every day for a year: the bliss of the hunt,
fine music, great poetry, her dazzling conversation.
At night her baffled warmth behind him,
the silence crackling between them,
his face to the bedroom wall.'

He can hear the mutter along the benches.
Let the story come to you.

'Soft as the turn of the tide,
or a subtle shift in the wind,
the body knowing time
before the brain can register.
A herald arrives with the formal challenge.
He rides out to the ford.
A shallow river with low banks, fading
towards the trees on either side.

The kingdom has turned out to see the duel.
Two armies facing across the water,
rippling rows of shields clicking together in the wind,
banners, a hedge of spears, light flicking on steel,
self-important heralds to ensure no interference
while the single combat lasts.

On the other bank, his enemy
dangerous as a toy soldier,
anonymous in armour.
The voice inside his head:
Shape shifter, trickster,
you have stolen my kingdom.
With God's help,
I will prove it on your body.

They clatter together though the shallows,
like old friends who haven't met for years.
He strikes the man from his horse,
with so little effort he's sure he missed.

Ah, Chieftain, said his foe,
a tangle of metal and leather spilled into the river,
what cause have you to hate me?
Why steal my wife and lands?
But since I'm dying, finish me off.
I may regret this 'til the end of time, said Pwyll,
but I will not strike another blow.
He dismounts. Removes the dented helmet.

His dying enemy is Arawn, King of Annwfn.

The riverbank's deserted.
On both sides the land fades
into an absence of trees or skyline.
The silence hurts him.
There is only the body in the water,
and the blood ribboning down the quiet stream.

He mounts and rides,
picking a path through the sudden trees
to the welcome layout of his hall.
His happy, yapping hounds, bounding around him.
His servants coming out to greet him.
Have you missed me, lads?
Of course Lord, a day without you
is a day without sunshine.

They all laugh together.
How long have I been gone?
Since this morning, Lord.
The other hunters have not yet returned.

She came to visit him each morning,
between sleep and waking,
when the mind's unhinged from its responsibilities,
and guilt is a daylight noun.
Clothes falling, the most desirable woman he's ever seen,
she smiles affectionately, amused, as she enters his bed
and all the things they hadn't done, they did.

There is a hill, and any prince who sits upon it
will see a marvel or receive a blow.
Pwyll confused, tangled in the time lapse,
remembering a face, regretting his courtesy,
travelling the obligatory circuit of his banal kingdom
welcomes the dare and climbs to the summit.

A rider, moving along the old road.
A slender figure on a huge horse.
A tune he's heard but can't name.
He sends a runner.
No matter how fast the boy,
the sedate rider moves away.

On the second day, he has a horse ready,
and the best rider in the court.

But though he flogs the horse
he cannot close the distance.

On the third day, the prince
takes the fastest horse he owns
and as the woman passes, follows.
The harder he tries, the faster he goes,
the greater the distance
though the horse he's chasing never
breaks from its ambling walk.'

Oh most beautiful of metaphors.

'Finally, feeling his horse about to fall,
he calls out: Lady!
In the name of the man you love the best,
please stop.

She is by his side, riding thigh to thigh.
It would have been better for your horse,
she says, if you had asked that earlier.
And he knows who she is before she lifts her veil.
The wife of Arawn, King of Annwfn.
The woman whose bed he shared.
And the prince he met in the forest.

You used me to kill your husband.

He was winter without hope of spring,
Cruel, selfish, protected by powerful magic.
My people suffered. Now they insist I marry.
My kingdom is at risk until I do:
not one of them will hold the ford for me.

What is this to me, lady?

You did not have to treat me
with consideration or respect.
If I could choose a husband,
I'd choose you. Lady, said Pwyll,
and there was not one part of him
that was not filled with love for her.
There is nothing I'd like more.

The sunsets in Annwfn on the theatre of her bed.
Clothes falling, the most desirable woman he's ever seen,
she smiles affectionately, amused, slipping under the covers,
and all the things they hadn't done, they did.
Like a stumbling horse,
an abrupt twist and fall to revelation.
Undressing not for him.
              Another man is waiting in her bed,
while his broken body lies forgotten at the ford.

My love, she said, are you unwell?

Lady, said Pwyll, stopping his horse.
I will not die like all the others;
metal and meat, rust and blood
washed by the waters of the ford.
Not for the pleasure of your company,
the promise of your body,
or all the riches of your kingdom.

Oh foolish man, she said,
and he was alone on the road.'

7

Ygrayne, listening to the story,
enjoying Gwydion's variations,
smiles at his suggestion that a man

could learn from his mistakes
and turn his back on power and sex.
Of course the prince was not surprised
another man might offer him his wife,
and the wife would not be outraged
to learn that he had made the offer.

Gorlois. Her husband.
The hostages he sent,
are the sons of men he doesn't trust.
They will abandon him first shift in the wind.
He has never learnt the art of making friends,
safe behind his ring of forts, convinced
that being right is all that matters,
perpetually surprised that being right
converts nobody to his cause.

This Uther is magnificent.
Listening to her husband,
she had expected a psychotic dwarf;
stupid, brutal and incompetent.
But his people love him.
He draws them to him.
He is at ease in the moves a king must make.
Someone as hard as Urien will die for him.
His killer son, the one they call the Reaper,
won't cross him. There is only one result.
They have wilfully stepped on board a ship
that everyone knows will sink
and all they can do is play their parts
until the wreck goes down.

That curious masculine desire
to win the world's approval
by the manner of your death
and so be worthy of a song.
All these boisterous corpses

eager for the opportunity
to show how casually
they will throw away their lives.

If Gorlois loses what will Uther do?

She knows what happens
to the wives and daughters
of defeated chieftains.

A white rag dragged along the benches.

When Gorlois loses.
But a king like Uther needs a queen.
How to unpick him from that girl at his side
who plays the wife, but can never be the bride.

Chapter Six. Dunian

Octa and Ebissa, Hengist's aging sons,
between the stone wall and the turf,
accumulating warriors,
hearing of Hengist's death
gathered their kinsmen
and plundered their way south.
York's Roman walls were no defence
against trickery and cunning.
No more scattered landings
along the southern coast:
the Humber became an artery
to the bloating heart of Saxon York.

Poison had seen to Aurelius,
and Uther had raced
along the road that led from London.
But in haste, with half his army
and he watched it destroyed
in a single engagement.
His mounted warriors
crashing and tumbling,
horses and men, crumbling
against a line of shields
hedged with massed spears.
Vortigern had taught them well.
They held their line and the Britons fled,
through the woods to the hill of Dunian,
hiding amongst the boulders
on its wind smashed slopes,
watching the Saxons making camp,
taking their time, knowing
that in the morning
they would flood up the hill
and kill them all.

Uther sits by a fire made of twigs,
in a space between two boulders,
and dozes, waiting for his captains
to count the men he can command.

Gwydion sits on the edge of the light.

'I saw you and your men,
slaughtering Saxons
til we were safe in the trees.
I had you for a dreamer.'

'I dreamt their deaths,
and my dream became their reality.
Dreamers can't be men of action?'

'True. No doubt there is a story.
Make it brief.'

'A story of Brutus,
when he was a young exile,
in his sleek black ships,
scanning the horizon,

lost and desperate for water.
They landed on an island,
more a tree crowned rock,
abrupt cliffs, vertical, grey,
splintered with green,
and a faded path, leading
steeply from the only beach.'

'I know this one' said Uther,
ignoring Gwydion's irritation.
'It's a family favourite.
They find a cave, and in the cave,
there's a pool of water,

and by the pool a statue of Diana,
with a lion curling round her legs.

Oh foolish man, she said,
father-killer, vagrant, exile,
to find your home you have to travel
to a place your fathers never knew.
Then she promised him this island.
Know it well.
Gets trotted out on a regular basis.'

'What you haven't heard,
is what he left out, what
he told his chief bard,
on his death bed.

After the goddess
had exhausted him,
and promised Britain,
the lion of stone began to speak;

Betray her trust, and your descendants
will be erased by those more worthy.
The little evils that your family do,
the petty crimes of lust and malice
accumulate until the final treachery
when nephew and uncle kill each other
by a nondescript river.
Its name will become a synonym
for catastrophe, treachery, death.

You're the last of the line.
You have no nephews.
I see no river down below.
This is not where you die.'

Gorlois is standing over them.

'Tell me, Uther Pendragon,
why do you sit here in the cold
when our enemies are sleeping,
well-fed and warm?
I will take my men and attack their camp.
If we are silent, we can be amongst them,
before they wake and arm.'

Uther stifles a yawn and wonders why
some men want to claim the obvious
as their personal property.

Gorlois has taken control.
'Pass the word. Leave the wounded.
If we fail and they survive the cold
the Saxon spears will cure their ills.'

'Lords,' said Uther, rising,
then pauses to extinguish the fire until

in the darkness there is only his voice and the wind.
'Gorlois, you will lead your men down the hill.
Urien, Owain, with me and the storyteller
through those trees to the right of their camp.'

'You'll spring the trap before it's set.'

'They won't,' said Taliesin. 'That man there,' pointing to Gwydion,
'has been a wolf. The fox is deaf and blind when he robs its den.
These men will move like the wind over the treetops,
unlike the softest of breezes on the stillest of days,
not a branch or leaf will be disturbed by their passing.'

'But first,' insists Gorlois,
ignoring Owain's laughter,
'each man must confess his sins.
Ask God for forgiveness.

When He sees us as we are,
He will reward us with victory.'

'If it helps,' said Uther, 'but in my experience
Gods close their eyes when the dying starts
and keep them shut 'til the killing's done.'

2

Dawn. Light firming night's vague outlines.
They stand amongst the storm-wrecked camp:
tumbled shelters, strewn gear, pinned bodies.
The Saxon host is corpses they won't bury.
Octa and Ebissa are not among the dead.

'I thank you,' says Uther, willing to be generous,
though he doesn't owe him anything.
Gorlois shrugs. 'You are the king.
This is the second time you've won a battle
and lost so many men you can't continue.'

As he walks away, Uther notices Gwydion.

'He's right.
I've lost the best part of two armies.'

'We all heard you give the order.
The cavalry was not to engage
until the infantry arrived.'

'I went hunting with untrained dogs;
assumed an order would be followed.
Who knew obedience was optional?

Where were you when Vortigern was king?
Whose side were on you on then?'

'Until that final battle
when everyone will have to choose.
Our loyalty is to that Britain
given to the House of Brutus.

He saved your Kingdom.'

'True, he did do that. Is he dead?'

'Some stories have untidy endings?'

'Do you ever give a straight answer
to a simple question?
Isn't a man's life more than just a story?'

Amongst the dead bodies,
the scattered weapons,
there's no one to reply.

3 An embassy to the north

Riders on the great north road,
hurrying through the ruined province.

Signs of wealth and power
in the horses they ride,
in the broaches that hold their cloaks,
in the weapons they carry.

But so few to see them.
They passed deserted villages,
untilled, untended fields.

One night, as honoured guests,
feasting in a walled fort, in a converted granary
now the long wooden hall of the man in charge,

they heard how men, women and children,
too weak to walk, had crawled from their hiding places
to eat the grass, and worse,
had dug into fresh graves looking for flesh.

There was a time when huts clustered together
surrounded by their fields and gardens,
offering a cautious welcome.
They encountered ditches, stockades, hostility.
The people fled at their approach,
or locked their gates and welcomed them with stones.

They met the Saxon leaders outside the walls of York.
Urien and Lot, Lord of the Northern Isles,
leading the British delegation,
with Gwydion as latimer.

But the Saxons were unsettled
like a herd of does
before the stags begin to rut.
Open warfare for the right to lead
was on the wind.

Octa and Ebissa, sons of a great father,
need time to rebuild their army.
They are ready to deal.
Their agreement with Aurelius
died with him.

Lot knows these are not the men
their followers are watching.
'King Uther greets you.
He offers you his friendship,
if you stay north of the Wall
and abandon York.'

A voice from the back.
'If this Uther wants York,
why doesn't he take it?'

Gwydion notes a man
who watches Hengist's sons
like a farmer wondering
if it's time to slaughter the pigs.

Colgrim. Beside him, Badulf.
The dissonance in the tent
Men who never met Hengist,
unimpressed by his sons,
disdaining their failures.

4 Meet the future

An opportunity to meet this man.
Schooled by the sea's indifference,
by storms, shipwrecks, winter's famine;
lotteries of loss and pain that make a life,
and leave nothing to stand against 'I want'.

This Colgrim has no vague ambitions,
or dynastic plans. He wants
to glut his need on the carcass of the province,
to live one day wanting nothing
before he's cut down by his rivals.

'Hengist's sons? They are the past.
Why ask for something we can take?

Tell this to your king; Time carries us to victory.
This winter we will feast behind the walls of York
while hungry warriors, eager for plunder,
sail to our gates. In spring, we will ride the tide,

and flood the rich lands of the south.
Your time is over Wealh. This time next year,
your corpse will be unburied,
or you'll be starving in some bolt hole in the hills.

A single sharpened stake,
no matter how strong,
does not make a palisade.
Tell your king we're coming for his head.'

Chapter Seven. York

The royal summons to the levy,
finds Gorlois at castle Dore,
a small ring fort, with the land
falling behind him to the valley of the Fowey.[25]
The ground, silvered by frost,
smokes as the sun hoists itself over the horizon.
The trees that line the river,
bloom as dark stains on the mist.
His is blind to the beauty of sunrise,
deaf to the sounds of the fort.

Uther the King.

He throws the summons in the fire.
An Uther is a slimy thing
that crawled into his brain,
slithers though his mouth
and ears and eyes,
to settle in his throat
sending grasping tentacles
to hook his heart and stomach,
leaking acid into every burning joint.

Now Uther this and Uther that,
the world gone gaga for a fool
who could bore for Britain
with his endless babble
about some skirmish with the Huns.
He'd want a Triumph next.

The year after he defeated Hengist,
he had been a hero to his people

---

[25] Pronounced Foy

The Duchy ran itself, and there was time:
her wisdom, perception, intelligence
approving everything he thought and said.
The gift of her body, the pleasures of her bed.

He rebuilt Tintagel for her.
A palatial residence on the cliffs,
and fortified a refuge on the island
reached only by a narrow bridge.

A place for love and relaxation,
pleasure and mutual passion
safe from the demanding world.
Even the birth of a daughter
had not diminished his affection.

Then Fortune cranked her wheel.
The sky collapsed; the earth gave way beneath him.

He had entered the sanctuary of her room,
expecting her to greet him as she always did,
moving towards him with the certainty of the tide.
Instead, a wary stranger watching him approach.

When he had finished, she had shrugged him off,
smoothed out her clothes and he had seen a Gorlois
reflected in her eyes: a slobbering monkey
grunting his way to the ridiculous orgasm.

She flinched when he appeared,
and only spoke if spoken to.
From eager lover to reluctant mattress.
Bewitched? Possessed?
No longer the woman he adored.

She would not refuse him.
But she turned his desire
into shame and confusion.

'I'm sending you away,' he'd said.
'I don't think so,' she'd replied,
hinting there were lords who'd follow her.
Her smile had set his mind slithering
to images of that body with which men,
how many, where, how often, when?
In the pornographic theatre of his bruised esteem
he watched her whore herself to every man she met.

He'd set a boy to follow her,
but when the boy reported
she had seen no one, he knew
she had corrupted him. Imagining
her lips and hands at work upon this innocent,
her could smell her on him.
The boy had been destroyed.

From infatuation to loathing.
Easy as stepping from one room to another.
The way her accent tinted certain words;
her habit of saying the same thing several different ways;
the way she checked her reflection in every polished surface;
reasons to despise her confused by memories of tenderness,
tangling his mind in labyrinths of misery.

He had listened to the whispering against her,
the bastard offspring of resentment and desire,
'til certainty and common sense slid along a chain of innuendo,
and found something he could grasp
to make her pay for his humiliation.

In her apartments in Tintagel
there was a locked door.
Whisperings of sorcery.
Malicious magic: midnight orgies.

How else could she be so successful?

Hoping for potions, spell books, alembics
to prove the rumours true,
so her death could be nasty and righteous,
he had arrived at night, tramping the corridors
with the officers of his court, armed men,
and eager courtiers hurrying in their wake.
She stood in the doorway, looking bored.
'Don't do this to yourself,' was all she said.

There was nothing but the light of their torches
on the clean blank walls.
No clothes, no trinkets, no alembics, nothing.
No secret doors, no hidden panels. Nothing.
Public humiliation in an empty room.

There was no sympathy for her.
She had played him for a fool
and who can love a champion
in the game at which they've failed.
But doubts about his judgement
became a disease spreading through the court.

He saw it in his officers, like dancers off the beat,
waiting for the qualification that never came.
Then the whispering, until three men talking
had to be conspirators. His life illusion shattered.
Neither help nor hindrance to the man who made him.
Waiting for the moment to be right,
when the stars aligned and all the variables were calculated.
Until waiting became a habit he could rationalise.

The woman he adored, shrinking from his touch.

Even the heroic victory over Hengist.
His planned withdrawal to the hill fort,
the master stroke that awed his critics.
Now those critics were whispering:
He hadn't known that it was there.

2

The sky's a brittle vacant blue.
Winter's in the wind.
Summer's wheel ruts cast in concrete
and the lords meet in Uther's tent.
The Saxons have refused to give up York.

Adolf of Gloucester, out of retirement (again)
to play the elder statesman, explaining
to men who have not lived in the Island:
'No one takes an army north in winter.'
If no one stops him, he'll be telling them
about the time it trapped him on the Wall.

'He's right', says Gorlois, interrupting
'but the Saxons will sit behind York's walls
and wait 'til spring. We can take them then.'

'No,' says Uther, 'in spring more ships,
more men. We take them now.'

Gloucester, insisting that he can't.
At length. Then:
'How can you feed an army?
Where will you pasture the horses?'

'We don't need to feed an army.
York has a winter's worth of food.'

Uther studies the crumpled map.
He knows the forts and watch towers
are ruins haunted by the desperate;
the towns walled shanties.
The only thing that matters is the roads
and all his scouts have said that they will serve.
He traces a route with his finger.

'If we go light, we can go fast and far.'
Looking up to smile at Urien,
whose smile breaks slower,
as he realises what's coming.

To his captains: 'Mounted men only.
Each man to bring provisions for three days.
No looting, no requisitions.
We go to save these people,
not to harry them.'

Gorlois, embarrassed by his own voice:

'What chance
       have mounted men
               against the walls
                       of York?
They couldn't break
       a wall of spears
               at Dunian.'

Suddenly in shadow, as Lot towers over him.
'Who did send our riders at those spears,
despite the king's orders, against the advice of his officers?
And who broke first and ran for the hill?'

'None,' says Uther. Gorlois exasperated,
but before he can speak, Uther continues, quietly:
'but the northern siege train,
the one built by engineers I brought from Gaul,
my siege train, left Lincoln a week ago.
They can only trundle.
They won't risk the direct route and the ferry,
but they should arrive before those walls
with their infantry escort, about the same time we do.

We will be feasting in York,
this time next week.'
Gorlois pushes his way through the excited captains.
The knowledge he has humiliated himself
folding him into his misery.

3

The frost is trampled,
the gaunt landscape fouled by men and horses.

York is smoking in the background.
A dirty smudge of walls and roofs.
On the river the fleet is burning
the masts like tree trunks in a bushfire
dark verticals breaking the orange flames.

The Saxon army traumatised
by the speed of its defeat
is lined up outside the shattered walls,
bound and on its knees
in the black ash drifting
like perverse snowflakes
from an empty sky.

Uther, mounted, looking down,
on two naked men kneeling in the dirt.
They have loaded themselves with chains.
Octa and Ebissa, in abject surrender,
their chieftains behind them in similar poses.
They are blue with cold but refusing to shiver.

Gwydion waits for the day to explode.
The silence is a terrible hinge.

Finally, Uther begins to speak,
with Gwydion translating.

'I have known some great men.

Men who were not names in a story;
men who changed history: Attila,
Aetius, Theodoric. I never met your father.
But he was one of them and he died,
to buy you time, so for his sake,
I will not kill you, now. Get off your knees.
Get dressed. I will take you as hostages
for your countrymen's good behaviour.

He waves towards the kneeling army,
'Kill them all,' turns to his officers.
'We will stay here for a week.
I will hang every man who harms a citizen.
And every citizen who harms or cheats
the lowliest of my men. And pass the word,
each man will be rewarded,
distribute the Saxons' women
and their horde amongst the army.
Give my share to the engineers
and those who worked the siege equipment.
Say York is theirs for three days.
By sunrise on the fourth, I want them out
and the siege train heading south.'

He turns to Gwydion,
to the sounds of bound men being slaughtered.
'A week to rest, and then I will go north,
to pacify the land between the stone wall and the turf.
By Easter I will be in London, for a proper coronation.
I expect to see you there. You still owe Ness her story.'

4 Merlin

Home for the dead king's magus.
An ancient stone tower,
wind battered, moon stained
on the rocky coastline.

At the top of the stairs,
a room lined with shelves
chaotic with scrolls.
Charts sprawl over the tables,
crisscrossed with hieroglyphs
and geometric symbols.

Stage dressing for the gullible.
He knows what they expect
but so few dare to visit
dust covers the ridiculous props.

He sits by the window
reading the night sky.
The one text he can read.

Time returns for the Hero King,
manoeuvring stars in their battalions
announce the alignment is auspicious.
His child fathered on the Golden Woman.
But Vortigern had thwarted him.
Denying him, denying her, perverting history.[26]

Now he stills himself
becomes the pivot of the world
beneath the spinning stars.
Only one track leads through the past to where he sits,
here, at this crossroads of now,

---

[26] See *A Man of Heart*. Chapter Nine

the paths that lead away
multiply and radiate
like the spokes of a lady's fan.
So many possibilities.
In one, he is immortal,
his name is spoken, shouted, sung
as long as there are voices.
The Path of the Hero King.
Without him, he is the echo of a tree falling
in a country yet to be discovered.

His birth must be a wonder
to suit the narrative's demands.
The paths split, merge, tremble
as Merlin feels his bile rising.
Should have been his son,
but the stars have shifted,
his moment's gone.
Now they demand the combining of others.
Uther? Of all the scum beneath the sky.
Like the roots of an enormous tree
fingering out through his life and history
finding only reasons for hatred and envy.
The paths explode as Merlin's anger flares.
His blinks, his room's in flames,
a movement of his hand, the flames are gone.
But not the bitterness or the sour craving for revenge.

He will arrange the birth of the Hero King,
and the destruction of Uther Pendragon.
Not the Pendragon, nor the King.
He will find the place where he feels safe,
and bleed the life out of the man.

5

Uther and Ness, in her rooms.
The maids absent. Gwydion enters.

'You were right.
He mustered his army before leaving for this feast.
Stuffed and garnished his many fortifications.
Though some of his tenants have sent their excuses.
He's ready for war. He's split his forces.
The crossings and roads are watched
but not guarded. He's not going to attack.'

'So tell me, Gorlois will arrive tomorrow.
What should I do with him? What would you do?

Don't look at me like that, girl.'

Uther manhandles Ness upright,
turns her to face Gwydion, 'These,'
pulling her dress off her shoulders,
'are the best tits I've ever kissed. And this,'
he slides the dress over her hips, takes
her hand and pulling it high above her head
uses his other hand to make her pirouette,
'is the finest body you'll ever see, but this'
he kisses her forehead,
'is the smartest person in the room.
So sharp she makes the wind bleed.
So when I ask for your opinion, lady,
it means I want to hear it.'

Gwydion, hating him, restrains the urge
to turn him into something he could tread on,
realising that Uther has not raised his voice
and there is a gentleness in his speed.
Their actions flow like a perverse dance.

And there's no fear on her.
She seems amused by his embarrassment.

He watches their staring match,
staring at Ness. The finest, indeed.
Oblivious to her lack of clothes,
she sits down on the bed.

'You can't have a vassal,
ruling a chunk of the kingdom,
treating the king with contempt.
Resistance is contagious.
Is he safe behind the Tamar?'

'Safe? I know how to take a hill fort.
Learnt the trick in Gaul.
Little time, few losses.
While my brother was getting educated,
I was learning the Roman art of sacking cities.

What? Did you think exile in Brittany
was an idyllic interlude?
Well, maybe for Aurelius,
he was next in line.
Me, I was just the spare.

My earliest memory? Waking up
to see a group of armed men,
blinding and castrating
the kind old man who cared for me
while some Breton raped my mum.

He was the first man I killed. I was six.
Mum was dead by then. An irrelevance.
But Aetius wanted the Bretons to counteract the bagaudae.
When he mustered, I went with him, a hostage in the imperial staff
seconded to the Gothic cavalry with Thorismund.

I fought at Châlons.
Did you know that?
Best day of my life.[27]

A million men, scared stupid, screaming,
in god alone knows how many different tongues,
blade on blade, like water dripping on my forehead,
or the sky being hammered open because the dust obscured the sun.
It looked as though the plain dissolved and flowed towards us,
ten thousand Hun cavalry in a horizontal avalanche,
the noise coming up through your feet to rattle your teeth.

Our orders were to take and hold the ridge.
No way of telling who was who.
There were Goths with us, Goths with Attila,
Franks fighting Franks. Even Aetius didn't know
who his enemies and allies were.
I just killed anyone in front of me.
All day long. We slogged 'til it was dark,
and no one, not even Attila
knew if we'd won or lost. I remember,
the morning after, weeping with exhaustion,
so tired I thought I'd never ride again.
The flies were the sound of the world's migraine.
Do you know what half a million dead men smell like?

My parents, and both my brothers were murdered.
Would you bet against those odds?
One day I won't hear the assassin,
or see the point or edge that does me in.
So forgive me if I'm in a hurry.'

He touches her, tentatively,
for the first time since she sat down.

---

[27] The Battle of the Catalaunian Fields. Fought in 451. The size of both armies, and the number of casualties, though enormous, is unclear. Some medieval sources would agree with Uther.

'And crass at times.'

'Gorlois refortified Tintagel rock.'
Gwydion, watching as Uther fingertips her shoulder,
'Three men can hold that bridge.'

'But that works both ways.
If there's only one way in,
there's only one way out.
I can pen him there with fifty men
and ravage Cornwall.
Does wonders for a lord's popularity
when his people know he's snug at home
while theirs are burning round their ears.'

'Is the north secure?'

'From here to the turf wall.'

'What about the Church?'

'They think that Gorlois
sides with the heretics
and gives them shelter.
They want him gone;
a hard-line Bishop in the West;
armed men to back him.
If I approve their synod,
and supply the troops
they'll preach obedience
to the House of Brutus.'

'I thought you favoured the heretics?'

'While they're fighting over their imaginary friends,
I have a country to administer. And the Church
can provide me with literate administrators.'

'Colgrim and Badulf?
They fled from York.'

'Slunk home to lick their wounds.
They'll have to fight to prove they're still worth following,
then raise a fleet. They won't be back this year or next.'

'You tried gracious.
If you have to fight him, fight.
But if you fight him, make sure
you're the aggrieved party.
Make sure the British lords
are sympathetic to your cause.
Otherwise, win or lose against Gorlois,
you lose in the long run.
Some think he saved you at Dunian.'

'Gorlois isn't your only problem.'
They both turn outwards,
surprised that Gwydion is still there.

'Not Gloucester, surely?'

'His wife.
Scheming for her survival and her daughter's.
More influential with the tribal leaders
than her husband. Gwendoline's game:
a favour here, a land grant there.'

Aestrild and her daughter,
slack jawed, smiling at Ness,
move the shadows closer.
Heb dan heb wely.
wylaf wers. tawaf wedy.[28]

---

[28] Without a fire, without a bed, I will weep and then be silent. See *A Man of Heart* Chapter One.

Their cold touch tightens her face.
She reaches for her clothes
to hide her reaction.
'You should kill her too.

Why do you look at me like that?
You could have Gorlois assassinated.
But no, you'll march an army into Cornwall
and hundreds of men who've done you no harm
will line up to die as their homes are destroyed.

Do you think those Saxon girls
you casually doled out to your soldiers
were treated with kindness and respect?
Did you stop and consider the horror you inflicted on them
with a few words mixed in with all your other words?
Can you imagine the terror of their final hours?'

If you wait, thinks Gwydion,
the ice on the river will break,
and what has been hidden
will surface and be visible.
Knowing that what she says
could easily be translated.

There is an obvious solution to their problem
and none of them wants to speak it.
Her fears are real but none of them
want to address them either.

'The western lords don't want to fight.
They mustered and died for Gwendoline,
but they worshipped her father
and treated her like she was their daughter.
This girl's a blow in on the tide.
They'd rather follow you than Gorlois.'

'Storyteller, would you leave us?
I wish to speak with Ness in private.'
He is used to the way they coil together,
before he has shut the door,
and their bright unforced laughter,
runs after him along the corridor.

But now they sit like baffled diplomats
facing each other across a treaty
neither wants to ratify.
The only sound in the corridor
is the painful echo of his foot fall.

Ness alone, prowling her room,
stops to stare at the mirror.
Some whey-faced Cornish Bitch
with her tiny waist and her perfect tits.
What can she do for him
that I haven't done whenever
and where ever and how ever
he wanted?

'The western tribes,' says Aestrild.

The room is empty
But at the reflection's edge,
Aestrild and her daughter
are growing firmer in the shadows.

Turning from the mirror
She hears them speak
soft, like the tide on the sand.

'He must do what he must do
to secure his kingdom.'

For sale then, one previous owner.

Chapter Eight. Second Crown Wearing

1

A delegation of self-important men,
hunched into Uther's displeasure.

'My lord, your happiness is our desire,
but you have no son. Without an heir,
the country is condemned to civil war.
Please, take a wife, secure the succession.'

'You have some body in mind?'
A babble of names. Faces he recalls.
Daughters of ambitious fathers.
And if she's stupid or clever,
plain or pretty, gentle or vicious,
what matters is how many men
follow her father into battle.

'Give me a year. Let me solve
our military problems. Then,
we shall discuss this properly.
Otherwise there will be nothing to inherit.'

2

Merlin,
striding across farmland
like a moving stain.
There is a farmer's daughter.
Cleaned of the reek of cattle
she'll do for tonight.
Her sister is in service with Ygrayne.
She wants a place at Uther's court.

Lies, flattery and attention;
he can be that doting lover.
The silly girl won't have the sense to see she's being used.
He will obtain the ingredients his spell requires.

Her gullibility will ensure it is delivered.

3

Adolf of Gloucester,
Killer of Hengist, loser of armies,
elderly, portly, growing bald.
Requesting a private audience,
with Ness and Gwydion as witnesses.

Beyond his rank or personality
he carries a residual dignity,
like the sole survivor who swam ashore
after Atlantis was destroyed.

He creaks onto his knees,
then offers his sword, hands shaking.

'Old age, my king, not fear.
Who will stand before God
on the day of judgement
and say *I have not* sinned?

If war comes in the west,
I will not fight the House of Brutus.
Accept my homage, accept,
whatever I can offer that you want or need.
If the Vicarius had appointed me,
I would have welcomed you home.'
(Which they all know is a lie,
but as Ness will argue later,
his oath seems genuine.)

4

His broken nose, his scarred face,
his awkward movements, betray
a long life in the saddle
hacking and being hacked.
This is Urien. The tall timber
beside him his ferocious son,
Owain, a killer by choice.
Crazed, addicted to cattle raids.
Stealer of other men's wives.
Taliesin calls him:

'A reaper of foes, a predator'.
This, of course, the highest compliment.

'Urien,' says Uther, coming off the throne to greet him,
'before my brother mustered his army,
you had been loyal to me.
The land between the walls is yours.
Fortify the rock of Edin, make it your home.
Make sure the Saxons don't come south.
You can have what's left of York as well.'

Urien bows. 'My king is very generous.'

'Your friend pays his debts.
I will miss you at court
but know the north is safe.'

5

Uther at the high table.
An empty seat
where Ness usually sits.
He wears his crown.

Gorlois has left his arrival
as late as possible, again.

He is flanked by men who Uther knows,
officials from his brother's court.
They flutter in the duke's wake
like moths chasing a moving light.
Gorlois strides to the high table.

'These men have a story to tell
about the death of your brother.'

They are trying to hide in plain sight.

'When the Lord Aurelius was ill,
Appas your personal physician came to us.
He poisoned your brother, our king.'

Words spoken so softly
provoke a violent reaction.
Urien has drawn his sword.

Owain is moving towards Gorlois.
Uther pacifies them. 'My doctor?
Appas? That sounds Saxon.
Why would I have a Saxon doctor?

Tell me, did he have my seal?'

'He told the gathered lords,
and the dying king
that you had sent him.'

'Not one of you checked or challenged his credentials?'

'He gave us cinnamon, liquorice and ginger.'

'How much did he charge?'
'Nothing. He said:

Hider me sende Vther; þe is þin aȝen broðer.
& ich al for Godes luue; æm to þe her icume.
for ich þe wulle helen; & al hal makien.
for Cristes leofe Godes sune; ne ræche ich nane garsume.
no mede of londe; no of seoluere no of golde.
ah ælche seocken ich hit do; for luue of mine Drihtene.'[29]

'You trusted a doctor who didn't ask for payment?'

Whatever had carried them this far,
is not enough to take them any further.

'Would you recognise him again?'
On their knees, trembling, they nod.
'Send for my doctor.'

They all agree that this is not the man.
Gorlois is outraged.

'They do not know him.
Wait', said Uther,
'this could be another trick.
How many here recognise my doctor?

We thank you for your concern,
but is it not the easiest thing
to pretend to be someone
when no one knows the person
you are imitating.'

---

[29] Lines 8836-8841 Laȝamon's *Brut*. In the *Brut* no one blames Uther despite Appas' claim that he was sent by him.

6

The cup bearer takes the cup from the maid,
and brings it to Uther. Who watches as the servant,
sips, waits, nods, then gives the cup to him.
He's watching Gorlois walk back to his place.
The room shifts as though he's on the deck
of the ship that brought him back to Britain.
He hands the cup back. 'I think your wine is off.'
How austere the lines of her face, how dark her eyes.

Uther is polite and formal, dignified,
knowing it irritates his guest.
He watches Gorlois seething.
He is waiting for an excuse to explode
and hunker down behind his river boundary
pretending he's in charge and the world hasn't changed.

But Uther plays the perfect host, thinking:
the Roman Art of Insurrection?
Another Maximus on the make?
What does he know of the Imperial world?
The backstabbing, money grubbing,
office grabbing, murderous, treacherous
world I grew up in? Lord sitting on his arse
watching his patron demolished?

'My Lord', says Urien, 'are you unwell?'

He has seen so many lovely women.
Why the sudden drag towards this one?
A ship driven inexorably onto a lee shore.

He rises to mingle with his guests,
then stops, by accident, beside Ygrayne.
'Lady, would you grace me with your company?
I would know you better.'

She takes the offered hand, rises, walks beside him.
The formal elegance of dancers.
Gwydion, watching closely, as
Uther offers her the empty chair beside him.
She smiles, and he smiles,
and while they find something to talk about,
it's noisy in the hall, so they lean together.
Uther lightly touching her arm,
signals for the cup bearer,
who drinks first to test for poison.

They both drink from the same cup.
He brushes a stray hair from her face.

It's like watching a sea cliff finally collapse.

Gorlois is on his feet, raging,
storming the high table:
'You will not have my wife!'
He's waving a knife at Uther.
A child threatening an adult with a toy.
'You are no king of mine.
You are not fit to wipe the arse of my stable boy.'

Ygrayne, horrified, dragging at his arm.
Uther standing, bellowing, 'Sit down.'
Gorlois is hauling his wife towards the door.

'Sit down! I do not give you permission to leave.'

The men of Cornwall, backing out of the room,
wishing they had not left their weapons outside,
form a ring around their leader and his furious wife.

Uther, strangely calm for a man so insulted,
waits for the other guests to settle.

'My Lords, judge me, have I done wrong?
The duke misread my actions.
You all know there is only one woman in my life
to whom I am devoted,
the most loyal husband in all but name.'

Nodding heads. He's loyal to Ness.
They wish he weren't.
She's the reason he won't marry.

Few were watching, those who were
confirm that there was nothing untoward.
They've seen public seduction.
Uther's father and eldest brother
were shameless practitioners of the art.

This was courtesy and nothing more.

Uther to Urien:
'Please, go remind the duke
it is a capital offence
to commit affray in the king's presence,
or to leave without permission.
If he returns, I will pardon both insults.'

'And if they don't, my king?'

The assembled lords are muttering again.
How would anyone dare insult Uther
and then refuse his offer of a pardon?

'My lord,' says Lot, 'I speak for those assembled here.
If he will not return, we will follow you to Cornwall,
and break him on the walls of his fortress.'

Triumphant agreement along the benches.

7

Urien finds the Cornish
in the confusion of the stables,
in the haste of unplanned departure,
saddling to ride.

'Gorlois, calm down and come back.
The king has no lust for your wife.
You have insulted him.
Come back and apologise.
He has publicly announced
he will pardon your gross behaviour.'

'Tell your fratricidal lord,
he will never touch my wife again.
Tell him, neither duke nor duke's wife
will be returning to this court.
Tell him if he wants me
he knows where I am.'

Chapter Nine. To Tintagel

1

They plundered their way into Cornwall.
As they crossed the Tamar, unopposed,
and left the Roman roads,
unseasonal rain, becoming biblical,
turned the tracks to slime.
Uther's siege train stalled and sank.
While Tintagel was invested
he led the army against Gorlois,
who huddled in his hill fort.
But they had to wait for the bogged machinery
as creeks and rivers, flooding,
tried to liquify their camp,
with the great hill and its rippling banks
lowering over them in the murk.

Urien, hurrying Gwydion to Uther,
slopping though the mud
that flowed between the tents.
They stop at the entrance.

Uther, still as a monument,
slack mouthed, vacant.
The skin of his face dragged taut
below the dark hollows of his eyes.
The royal doctors arguing.

'Behold, his looks and colour
few would recognise him.'

'Lord,' said Gwydion, 'what ails him?'

'The doctors can't decide.
Amor Morbus, driven mad by lust.
Some think he is bewitched: others poisoned.
He hasn't mentioned Châlons for a week.
He talks incessantly and incoherently
about the duke's wife.
He's fading so quickly they don't think
he'll see tomorrow's sunset.

You can undo this.'[30]

Pride is a seductive god.
It flares now, beckoning him,
replaced by the feel of a rusted saw
scraping on a bone,
resonating with a memory.

A boy, ravaged by insomnia.
Wasted to bone,
bleached by care.
All for her love.

And what happened next.

But an off note. Like a tune
played skilfully on a harp
with one string flat.

'Did he send for me?'

---

[30] When Geoffrey of Monmouth was writing this story, 'Love Sickness' was entering European medicine as a recognisable medical condition. See Wack, Mary F, *Lovesickness in the Middle Ages*. People have believed in love potions throughout history. They can still be bought online. For an entertaining discussion see the relevant chapter in Harvey, Katherine, *The Fires of Lust; Sex in the Middle Ages*.

'No. He's sent for Merlin.
But you're his friend,
I know that you can fix this.'

'No.' Stopping in the entrance.
'Not again. I won't.'
But the sound of the rain,
like a river gone vertical,
and the erratic percussion
of water shaken from the roof,
flushes away his voice.

'Gwydion, I am bewitched.
I see her everywhere.
A room, a bed, her body.
How do I remember
what hasn't happened?

Find Merlin.
Why do my hands
remember her?'

He's not hard to find
when he wants to be found.

Reed like, but a new Merlin.
His clothes are finest gold brocaded silk.
His hair and beard are trimmed.
He looks like a scholar with ambition
stepping from a Byzantine icon
striding erect though the puddles,
refusing to bow his head to the rain,
with Owain two steps behind.

Uther, so distraught he can't speak.

Gwydion sees a carrion bird
with shiny feathers
gloating over a dying stag.
But the warlords recoil.

'The dragon is out of its cave
burning everything in sight.
Lust rampant, not caring for the object,
just the satisfaction of desire.'

'We have no time for riddles,'
said Gwydion, 'Uther needs you.'

'No, the poor lust struck fool
needs Ygrayne's body.
Nothing else will cure him.'

Uther, great energetic warrior,
gaunt, trembling with the effort
of sitting upright.

'You can see her can't you.
Those marvellous tits spilling free.
You remember them in your hands
and in your mouth
Those fine long legs…'

Gwydion staring into the vacancy
behind those speckled golden eyes:

'If all you're going to do is gloat,
I will nail you to the nearest tree,
and leave you there to rot
while all the people you've offended
queue up to piss on you.'

The boy steps back.
'I can turn you inside out!'

The warriors cower
expecting lightning bolts
to crash the sagging roof.

Gwydion smiles: 'No. You can't.'
Then he leans forwards and whispers in his ear.

'I am that Gwydion son of Don
who made a woman out of flowers,
turned a boy into a bird,
the bird back to a boy.
Compared to me, you
are a raindrop in this thunderstorm.

All you do is party tricks
to scare the children.
If you did this to him,
undo it. Now.'

The warlords see Merlin stagger
brushing at his robes.

'Didn't. Can't. Won't.'
But Gwydion is following him,
still so close he might be trying to kiss him.
Softer, so his voice blends with the rain.

'Think of the applause
when you save the king.
Think of the eternal story,
and your utterly undeserved role in it
as saviour, prophet, magus
herald to the Hero King
whose coming you foretold.'

He shakes himself again,
hiding his confusion by tidying his clothes

as Gwydion steps back, watching him.
(He reminded her of a hawk.)

'Uther king, someone bewitched you
ond Minheu a baraf.
You must come with me to Tintagel.
Bring this storyteller.
You will become the man you hate
to be the man she loves.'

2

Merlin leads on a fine white horse.
Uther rides between them,
slumped and swaying in his saddle,
like a sack of turnips on a carter's dray.
The rain has stopped
and an insipid evening mist straggles
across the undulating landscape.
A trackless waste, darkening.
Its sounds and smells, darkening.
Darkness forming in the hollows.
Dark birds on their homeward flight.
Dark shapes flitting over the tors
as the sun fades. Broken walls.
They cross streams in spate,
a line of stones,
small broken settlements,
old as the moors themselves,
home of tin miners who lived here
when Paris was seducing Helen,
whose descendants watched
as Gwendoline rode past
on her way to kill her husband.

A shape on the skyline.
Darkness in the darkness
defines itself to cromlech;
burial place of giants,
before Corineus killed them all.

The gash of the entrance
between two vertical stones.
'Remind you of anything, Uther?'
Merlin dismounts. Hands the reins
to Gwydion. 'Take the horses
to the entrance on the other side.
We'll meet you there.

You need to be Gorlois' steward.
If you can manage that party trick.'

On the other side of the hill
Gwydion was ambushed by the sea
stained all the muted colours of the sunset.
To his right, ragged cliffs and tiny bays,
outlined by the surf
confront the sea's restlessness.
Somewhere to his left, Tintagel rock,
magnet for tin traders since before Troy fell.

The sea and sky on fire.

Why attempt to rationalise desire?
Witchcraft, probably. Ygrayne or Merlin.
Together or alone?
Or lust running to excess.
If this were a story,
he'd take the simplest answer.

But character refused coherence,
and the plot line made no sense.
How could he explain it to her?

Ness? He's falling before he knew there was an edge,

'The finest…' oh yes indeed, the finest.
Delirious, incoherent,
that marvellous body that she wears.
(That strange performance
put on for him
but to what purpose?)

He imagines stepping from the room
and closing her door,
but on this lust driven ride,
he fumbles the lock.
The door won't shut,
trapping him in a clichéd fantasy of sex.
The line of her jaw, the fall of her dress.
Mind-blasted by the softness
touch the curve feel the weight
in the palms of his aching hands,
as the tide washes him off his feet
out of his depth,
and into the bottomless dark.

An improbable owl,
a faint wing stretched blur
swooping across his line of sight

Gwydion, giddy, wind,
Owl, owing, wave
Dingy, windy, owing

dingy, dying, growing?

You're not very good at this,
laughed Taliesin,
arranging his vowels and consonants
into complicated patterns

of alliteration and assonance
creating undiscovered links
between such disparate *thing*s.

For the first time he smiles.
He wasn't, but he didn't need
complicated rules to see
the great heaving fact of the sea.
It's endless, energetic give and take,
the smell of it on the breeze
the damp nocturnal, autumnal earth
his own sweat and the familiar
smoke-stained smell of wool.
Everything chimes.
The owl's wingbeat; the waves surge,
every *thing* itself and a part of some *thing* else.

Taliesin conducting the world's music,
dancing at the centre of his web of overlapping words,
holding reality steady while he watched it flow.
Wind and tide, cloud and wave,
revealing the secrets of time itself.

He too had been at home,
before he met her,
before the slow discovery
that he wanted her approval,
but no apology or atonement
could unharm the people he had harmed.
Math's final punishment
leaving him stranded,
like the great neither nor of Tintagel,
divorced from the land,
rejected by the sea.

3

In the corridors of his memory,
there is one door he avoids.
A royal door, whose every
scratch and splintered surface
is waiting to be recognised.
Tonight he's drawn to it.
His brother's hand upon the latch.

Why must memory return us
to shame and embarrassment?
Merlin's gobbing laughter:
a virtuous man or women
is just a man or woman
insufficiently tempted.

He slams the door.

'You're becoming a hypocrite.' The voice
of his brother's butchered ghost.
'A self-denying, self-applauding hypocrite.

We were two proud hawks,
running down our prey.
Those old men we admired

showing their heroic scars
to wide-eyed eager boys,
stories of taking what they desired

from those too weak to stop them.
Gwell yd lad nogyt ydolwch.[31]
Predator or Prey. Your choice.'

---

[31] From 'Canu Urien'. *Early Welsh Saga poetry: A study and edition of the Englynion*, Jenny Rowland. Rowland suggests 'It is better for you to strike than to supplicate.' At a stretch 'Better to strike than ask'.

'We had forgotten the Red Queen's mandate:
Better to trade than to conquer:
better to risk disappointment
for the possibility of mutual profit.'

'I am not the hypocrite.
I never saw a pretty girl
I didn't want to fuck.

Whichever god or gods
designed the female form,
proved divinity through its perfection.'

'But the one you couldn't have
was the one you wanted most.
And the one you wanted most
did not want you.'

'Did I care what she wanted?
Gwell yd lad nogyt ydolwch.
Predator or prey. Deer or Wolf.'

Products of an ideology
that trained its merlins,
in a time when everyone
was ally, predator or prey.

'You could have stopped me.
Instead you made it possible.
What does that make you?'

'Not good enough to be a man:
too conscious for an animal.'

His brother had charged into battle,
without armour, helmet, or shield.
He wasn't ashamed of what he'd done.
He smiled when he remembered her.

It was the judgement of his peers
the honking and the squealing
as he passed along the benches
that drove him to his suicide.

But yes, oh yes, the finest that he'd ever seen.
The play of wit and wisdom like light on water.
Why should I not desire to hold her in the dark
and trace the moonlit line from shoulder down to hip.
If I came to trade, and she were free to choose?

The owl again,
hunting,
answers his question.

He shifts.
                The light has failed.
What trick is being conjured in the barrow
and why is it taking them so long?
Transformation at the level of appearance was easy,
but since this was no costumed role play
assuming the other's memory and character
required some effort: two people shuffling
in a small box, fighting for the window and fresh air.
A struggle easily won but the steward's brain
was a cluttered room, his limited vocabulary
a welcome impediment to any further thought.

4

'And now,' said Merlin.
'Time for my party trick.
Drink.' 'You first,' said Uther.

They emerged from the barrow into the dusk,
with the great gate of Tintagel before them.

Gwydion, impressed by the transformation,
hears Uther-now-Gorlois calling out:
'Where is my porter? Open my gates.
Don't you recognise your own lord?'
and the drowsy porter,
fumbles the locks in his haste.
They rattle over the narrow bridge
into an outer court where panic swirls
like dead leaves caught in the wind.

Uther acts as though he's lived here all his life,
not even checking to see the expected groom is there
as he hands off the reins. The hunting dogs
fawn around his legs. Two stone stairways
lead towards shut doors and Uther doesn't hesitate.
He's halfway up the one he chose
when Ygrayne appears, framed by the arch.
Wife Unkempt. No jewellery no finery.
Her hair is loose.

'I have stolen away, for love
to spend the night with you, m'lady.'

Gwydion can see no joy
or surprise in her reaction.

Uther would have talked with the groom.
He'd know his name, recall a fact,
show interest, then pause
to enjoy the dogs' attention.
He would have settled the chaos caused by his arrival,
called for the garrison commander,
listened to what he had to say.
made sure everyone was comfortable,
moving smoothly to familiar tasks.
He would have known their names.

But Gorlois gives orders
from the top of the stair
to no one in particular.
'These men you know.
Give them wine,
hot peppered chops,
women for their beds.
We leave before the dawn.
Tomorrow Uther dies.'

The door closes
and Gwydion and Merlin
follow the porter.

Chapter Ten. Tintagel

The cold stone steps upwards
following fall and call and promise.
Her lamp light curves the wall
fumbles their shadows
caresses her hip, warming
a bared shoulder aching his hands.

A room, claimed, personalised.
Small objects he doesn't recognise.

This woman had friends
he knew nothing about.
People whose versions of her
cared nothing for her face
or the shape of her legs.

Lust flowing towards,
flesh driven to flesh,
ambushed by the thought:
she lived with people
who saw her everyday
and didn't want to.

The inevitable boy
helped him out of his boots,
took his riding cloak; disappeared.
Maids with hot water,
clean white towels,
and shameless curiosity,
loitered over their task.

Smoke rising from the brazier,
the smell a rusty gimlet
stabbing through his ear.

She put out the lamps,
leaving candle flame,
and glowing coals.

Gorlois-Uther knows how this will end.
On the rare occasions he braves this room
she will lie beneath him, dutifully inert.
Understanding unlocking the banal.
The maids watching him in disbelief.
The boy's surprise when he declared
he'd risked his life 'for love of her'.
Finally, she shuts the door
on the reluctantly departing servants.

'You're trembling?
Is my lord unwell?'
Her suppressed smile
as he bends over the bowl.

Too dark to see whose face reflected
in the steaming bowl of water,
dark shapes that might be petals
floating on the surface.

She steps out of her clothes.
Pale form sketched by frail light.
The candle flame sways in the breeze
rumbling the sea through the narrow window.

Form contoured, highlight and shadow,
drowned wraith breaking the surface
sinking back into its depths
gaining substance as the light moves.

Water spilling bowl clatter
rattling over the floor,
punctuated by the dull sound of bodies
coming together, falling on the bed.

and Ygærne læi adun; bi Uðere Pendragun.³²

Of all the seconds that constitute your life
this is the one you will remember,
returning to haunt the hours
making the moments turbulent,
with regret and pointless longing.

Þe king hire wende to; swa wapmon sculde to wimmon do.
& hæfde him to done; wið leofuest wimmonne.³³

There is no reluctance tonight.
She is like a hero in combat
trying to catch his lord's attention;
a mutual assault
when they have nothing to defend.

She had not been surprised.

Exhausted by his desperate persistence,
perhaps she sleeps and dreams
and finds herself alone, then
becomes aware he's over in the corner,
sitting against the wall.
Confused by shadows
it might be anyone. She blinks.
Can't focus. 'My lord?' ' Why,'
the not quite voice of Gorlois, 'why?
No respect and no affection?'
Whatever happens in this dream,
it cannot hurt her.
'How can we be equals
if I must be silent and agree?'

---

[32] Line 9505. Laȝamon's *Brut*.
[33] Line 9508-9. Laȝamon's *Brut*.

He is beside her, gazing
at the pale curving line of body
lit by the risen moon,
the dark flowing stain of hair,
the hollows of her face in darker shadow
suddenly broken as she opens her eyes,
smiles, shifts towards him.

Surely at the end of such a journey,
there must be some revelation.

Words scatter,
like craneflies,
disturbed in autumn grass.

No revelation. Only bodies on the bed.
Whatever name he uses or who the other.
How passionately they embrace, now or
in all the rooms they'll share. They will always
dress and go their separate ways.

Clouds of nondescript butterflies,
thoughts, rise, flutter, then fall.

He remembers Darius, how he lashed the Hellespont,
throwing shackles in the water to chain rebellious waves.

'You were born to be a great lord's wife.'
'A greater lord than that doomed fool.'

As they begin again. This is the dream
in which you dream you wake
but the world is not quite as it should be.
Perhaps he dozes and dreams
he's starting again, busy, clever hands.

This tower will crumble.
The window will become a home for birds.
Weeds will grow in the cracked redundant walls.

Inside the room, time stretches, slows, becomes irrelevant.
Outside, it marches towards sunrise
and their inevitable collision with other people's words.

Uther wakes to see a stranger standing over him.
Remembers he is Gorlois-Uther.
Beside him, in the early light,
the naked woman is astonishing.
She frets, stirs, but
Merlin's hands are knotting her
into a deeper sleep.
She turns over, settles, smiles.

2

The great gates slam shut behind them.
They scatter the gulls along the cliff top.
The wind, carrying the smell of the sea,
flicking the grasses at the land's edge
bringing its exuberant invitation.

The scraped blue of a cloudless sky.
The strident greens of the rain-washed earth.

In the distance, clutters of riders.
Groups of five, six, hard to tell,
straining towards Tintagel.
Uther nods towards them,
'Probably all that's left.'

A sudden shift.
Uther becoming Uther,

watching Merlin
but speaking to Gwydion.

'Told you I knew a trick or two for taking fortifications.
If you can't send armed men up a mud slide,
find a way to bring your enemy down.
There are few secrets in an armed camp,
and one beside a fortress under siege
leaks gossip like a broken, flooded drain.
A husband who is tortured by the thought
his wife is shagging every man she meets,
hears the man who he despises most,
has left to screw her, stupefied by lust.
Then fear and rage eclipse his common sense,
and he forfeits his one advantage.

One trick pony Gorlois lead his army out,
at night of course, into the trap
Urien and I had set for him.
And if I know my friend,
my enemy's table is now his footstool
and Gorlois' head is on a stick,
watching him eat breakfast in his fort.'

'Why not ride towards Tintagel,
then circle back and wait?
Why go to all the risk
of entering the castle?'

A damaged Uther, smug and arrogant:
'Because if he didn't come down.
I was going to tell him, in detail,
exactly what I'd done to his wife,
with his wife and where I'd done it.'

It might be convincing in a story,
but someone put a spell on him

or slipped him a love potion
that would have killed a weaker man.

'Those stones on Salisbury Plain,
the ones you brought from Ireland,
I've met grandfathers who prayed amongst them,
knowing their ancestors worshipped there.'

'I didn't say we brought them all from Ireland.
Just the most important ones.
Did you really make a woman out of flowers?'

Gwydion reached down,
pulled a strand of long grass,
and offered it to Merlin.
The grass became bird,
and Uther watched it dart away
flicking low over the cliff tops.

More riders dotting the green.
'They're about to tell your well-fucked queen
her husband died before you entered her
or the castle. She will be terrified.'

The idea delights him;
spiteful foul-mouthed little boy.
Golden child of a demented woman,
never grown into an adult.

Uther moved away, called Gwydion to him,
looked out to sea, watching the gulls
crowding the cliff edge.
No, not her. Not terrified at all.

She had not been surprised.

Night loiters in images he can't escape
like persistent supplicants tugging at his cloak,
insinuating he should race back to the castle
and drown himself in her embrace.

'I knew that I'd been glamoured.
But everything was flowing the right way.
Seemed worth the risk to let go and be carried.
I hoped you wouldn't watch me die.'

'Queen?
You were willing to destroy her reputation.
If Gorlois lived, you signed her death warrant.
And now you're going to marry her?'

'Secures the western tribes
and the continental trade.
Merlin says she conceived last night.
If it's a boy, will you foster him?'

'Why me?'

The shadow of Gorlois is gone.
'We're clinging to the Imperial wreckage,
like those Trojan exiles
scheming a homecoming,
knowing Troy had been erased.

Diana's words to Brutus?
*To find your own home
carry your household Gods
to a place your fathers never knew.*

He will have to reimagine the world.
So teach him but tell him stories.'

The gulls, the sea, and the wind.

'Now back to your hills, storyteller.
It's a long time since you've been home.'

'It's been my privilege to serve
and my pleasure to know you,
Uther, King of Britain.
Before I go, I claim my payment.'

'You've earned your weight in gold.'

'No,' said Gwydion, 'my request.'

'Make it. If it's in my power and doesn't etc etc.'

'Ness. Her independence.
And her weight in gold
so she won't have to beg.'

The gulls. The sea. The wind.
And Uther, silent, watching
the gulls. The sea. The wind.

'Is this your way to redemption?
She told me your story.
Weren't you punished enough?

How long do you think she'll survive
alone, without male kin?
How long before her guards realise
no one will avenge the lady in the tower?

Ness, and my blessing, if you marry her.
Otherwise, I'll have to find a husband.

Ask her. Free to choose, she'd choose you.'

The gulls and the sea and the wind.

'I wanted to. Marry her.
I braved the cesspit of his court
to ask my regal brother
for his royal permission.
Marshalled all my arguments.
She would have made a queen
for history to marvel at.
Astute, honest, intelligent,
ruthless when she had to be.

I never got the chance to make my case.
He made the usual foul jokes,
then said: We marry for dynastic reasons.
Who is her father? What is his kingdom?

I'd never asked for anything.
Saved his life, done his dirty work,
but he said no and he was king.
And he was right. The royal family
are not private individuals
but must fulfil the obligations of their role.

You can't choose the story you're born into.
But I had stumbled into the miracle:
that Fabled Third that Brutus talked about.[34]
I was that Lucky Man. Gods roll the dice,
who understands the way they fall?

Then to be told I cannot,
may not, must not,
will not live my life with her?

To make a childish point
I stormed out of his court,
without his royal permission.

---

[34] See *A Presentment of Englishry* p.60

I thought of taking her to Gaul.
I still had friends there
and Thorismund was in my debt.
But then to prove his Royal Point
he sent me on an expedition
to steal some Irish rocks.
Just in case I failed to read the lesson
he sent him to accompany me.'

After they had trashed an army,
captains round the fire,
passing the drink.

Familiar faces in the firelight.
Subdued survivors blessed today by Fortune,
bound by stories, settling into silence

Around them the sounds of a military camp,
as Uther returns from visiting the wounded.
Merlin, sober, in his finery, excluded,
stands. 'You all despise me!
I have put up with your sneering jibes,
but I was there when the Morning Star fell.'

'Yes, yes,' said Owain, 'you loosed Leviathan
and harnessed the unicorn to the plough.
You can bore the bollocks off a bull but
you're useless when it comes to slaughter.'

'I predict the future.
I give Kings their orders.'

'What orders did you give my brother?'

> Time stops, the night stills,
> and brave men shrink backwards,
> trying to hide behind their shadows.
>
> 'He said no, didn't he.'

I didn't kill Aurelius.
When Aetius mustered the Bretons,
I went with him. One day,
he came to me, the man himself,
showed me a letter he'd received.
Aurelius and his advisers,
making it clear, in flawless Latin,
it would not displease them
if I were to meet with a fatal accident.

He said, "I can't protect you.
There's a thousand men in this camp
who'd rape their father if the price were right.
I'm sending you to Thorismund.
You have the gift of making friends.
If the Goths don't kill you:
you'll be safe with them."

The insults. The arrogance.
The times I saved his life.
A king who never led an army into battle,
who only ever got blood on the bottom of his boots?
Then ask not if I killed him but why I didn't?'

The birds, the sea and the sky
don't offer any answers.

'Loyalty, Honour, Duty
have to mean more than the crying of the gulls.

I knew a killer had been sent.
My messenger arrived after he was dead.'

Merlin, no longer sulking,
re-joins them, chuckles:
'But Gwydion, was the messenger delayed,
or did our king keep him waiting
until he knew it was too late?'

Chapter Eleven. Pay the Piper

1

Uther moved his army to Tintagel,
parked his siege train on the cliffs,
organised a demonstration
that the rock was well in range.

The survivors of the Cornish army,
unwilling to die for no good reason,
would have sneered at the suggestion
a man's wife could rule when he was dead
but eagerly obeyed the Lady Ygrayne
when she suggested they agree to Uther's terms.

He re-entered Tintagel
and no one else noticed
how familiar he was
with its internal layout.
And no one was surprised,
if, after the feast,
after the music and poetry
after the songs and carousing,
when the time came for them to sleep,
he took her by the hand
and lead her to her room.
His lack of hesitation,
making confession redundant.

He sent messengers to the western tribes.
If they came to him and swore their oaths,
he would treat them as his friends.
No need to outline the alternative
if they refused.

Days judging claim and counter claim
in the Ducal court,
listening to merchants and traders,
tolls, taxes, profit and loss.
Ygrayne beside him, how much she knew,
how shrewd her judgement.

A revelation.
Nights beside her,
no magic here,
the drag of a mutual
(conveniently self-serving)
fascination.

For the gossiping lords and ladies,
the drinkers at the benches,
cooks in the kitchen, boys in the stable,
it made a better story if the king,
lust driven, killed the duke to bed Ygrayne,
than the boring fact of a royal need
to secure the allegiance of the west
and control the continental trade
in luxury imported goods.

2

The naked woman in the mirror
watches as the woman in the room
rises from her bed, stretches then
collects her clothes. Knowing
they are safe. Knowing
she doesn't need the mirror.
The king's delight confirms her beauty.
Affection, intelligence and humour.
An interesting and interested man.
Loyal as well, if she gave him reason.

The naked woman in the mirror waits.
She need never be scared again.

But to eat the bull and choke on its tail?

Reluctance? Now? To risk so much
to reach the river and turn back on the bank?
Step into the breath stealing cold,
gripping rough stones beneath bare feet
resisting the logic of the current's force,
anchored by the horror of her thought
clutching like the cold, shrinking her into herself.

Then she gives in and lets the current take her.
The woman in the room hugs herself.

Then nods. There can only be one queen.

3

Mynet a oruc y mab ar Orwyd.
Off went the boy on a fine-looking steed:
grey-headed, shell-hoofed, four winters old.
A tubular gold bit in its mouth,
and under the lad a golden saddle.

In his hand two whetted silver spears
and a battle axe, its blade from edge to edge
the forearm's length of a full grown man,
so sharp it would draw blood from the wind,
swifter than the swiftest dew drop falls
from stalk to the ground in the month of June
when the dew is heaviest.

A gold hilted sword on his thigh, the blade
gold inlaid, a gold chased shield on his back,
with an ivory boss the colour of lightning.

A purple cloak was on him.
At each corner an apple of red gold,
each apple worth a hundred cows.

Two white breasted brindled grey hounds before him,
each with a gold collar from shoulder to ear
and the one that was on the right would be on the left
and the one on the left would be on the right,
like two swift terns, frolicking about him.

Four clods of earth were struck by the steed's hooves,
like four swallows in the air about him,
sometimes in front, sometimes behind,
but never a single hair stirred on his head
so sure and light footed his steed's canter
on the way to where Ness waits in Uther's caer.[35]

'My lady, there's a prince outside the gate,
he says he brings news of the king.'
'Send him in child, send him in.'
'He says you must go out to meet him.'

She takes two maids for modesty,
and seven guards for safety.

He has stepped out of the shadows
in the trappings of a prince.
A role he can inhabit without effort.
The busy traffic at the gates

---

[35] From Mynet to Caer is my adapted translation of lines 60-81 of *Culhwch and Olwen,* edited by Rachel Bromwich and D. Simon Evans, University of Wales Press, 1992.

shoal around him and his escort:
well-dressed, well-armed, well-mounted.

She came out with a fine silk
robe of flaming red around her
and at her throat a torque of gold
studded with pearls and garnets.
Her hair was blacker than midnight in a cave.
Whiter was her skin than the foam of a wave
on the clearest day of brightest sunshine.
Whiter were her palms and fingers
than the shoots of the marsh trefoil
thrusting through fine gravel by the clearest spring.

Neither the eye of the mewed hawk
nor the eye of the trice mewed falcon
was brighter than hers.
No breast of a white swan was whiter than hers
and her cheeks were as red as the foxglove.[36]

He greets her, enjoying her surprise
and the fact that there is joy in it.

'Lady it is you I love.
Come away with me.'

'That I cannot,' she replies.
'It would bring shame
and death upon us both.'

'No, Lady you are free.
Uther has killed Gorlois and taken Cornwall.
The Lady Ygrayne is with child.
She will become his queen.'

---

[36] From 'She came… to foxglove' is my adapted translation of lines 487-498 of *Culhwch and Olwen*. Olwen is a blonde and Ness isn't.

'You owed me a story.
Was that the best that you could do?'

She turns to quiet the distraught maids
who know their lives are ruined by her fall.
He offers her the reins he's holding.
'A fine white palfrey, fit for a lady,
and two ponies for her maids.
And the gift of Uther's blessing.'

Ness, outraged.
'You bought me with a story.'

With no idea what she will do,
he offers her the reins again.
'I brought you a choice.'

4

Smoke plumes on the horizon
interrupt this story he's telling himself
on the ride to Uther's Caer.

Outriders coming back
with women, children
and three of Uther's men.
'I swear,' said the damaged man,
'Britons. They came in daylight.
The gate was opened.'

He recognised the young man
now nursing a shattered arm
as the boy he'd threatened
to turn into a mouse.

'I saw you! We all saw you!
I will swear we all saw Uther
and you, and Merlin
with an escort like these
outside the gates.
I recognised his voice, calling out:
"Where is my porter? Open my gates.
Don't you recognise your own lord?"
The Lady Ness and her maids went out to him.'

Gwydion is flogging his horse,
the flames of the caer lighting his path.
Riders racing to the edge of the trees,
then the clearing, the smoking ruins.

A string of people passing buckets from the nearby river.
He rushed past, through the gates,
past the pile of bodies heaped outside.

He found her in the wreckage of the living quarters.
Smoke blackened walls, charred furniture,
Three bodies in the wreck.

Refusing to imagine their last hours,
he wished he were a wolf again,
threw back his head, began to howl.

Chapter Twelve.
The Education of Arthur mab Uthr [37]

1 Colgrim making History

The sky thick with clouds and darkening,
the humped skyline like a building wave,
a solitary figure snags the eye.

Over the chain mail, fur for warmth.
Over the furs, thick woollen cloak.
Everything as functional as the edge of his sword.

Below him in the wooded valley,
tents dot along the stream.
British lords, waiting to talk,
nervous as priests at the door of a brothel.
Hidden behind him, armed men,
tired, cold and hungry, waiting for his decision.

Badulf, scheming for a future,
that doesn't interest Colgrim,
had argued for patience, cunning
and permanent conquest.

Would you die for your children?

Now Badulf joins him, waiting.
Note the broach at his shoulder,
gold inlaid with garnets,
a masterpiece of the smith's art.

---

[37] Uther is not an historical character in the way Vortigern might have been, or Germanus was. One suggestion is that he was inspired by a mistranslation. Arthur mab Uthr, or a variant, could mean Arthur son of Uther, but it could also mean Arthur the terrible child.

He has dynastic ambitions.
Hengist's son, baffled by long captivity,
hands soft, muscles slack, minds locked
like a ship held head to wind,
irrelevant but useful. Let them fight Uther.
Whoever wins will be weaker, easy pickings.

Colgrim has no interest in widows
or the daughters of dead kings.
But he is hungry. 'We go down,'
he shrugs. 'The wælas can feed us
while they're selling their island.'

2 The Storyteller and the Poet

A visit from young Taliesin,
to drink Gwydion's mead,
and talk gossip and craft.
Neither a day older
than the last time they met.

'Have you heard Aneirin's latest?
Bit repetitive if you ask me.'[38]

'True, 300 variations:
A brave man. He fought. He died.'

'But it sings, Gwydion, it sings
and every declaimer has learnt it
and every bard is trying to make his own.

How can I make praise poems for Uther?
The man is astonishing.
He's brought us years of peace,

---

[38] The poem they are discussing and which they parody is *Y Gododdin*.

prosperity, the rule of law.
The farmer to his field.
The merchant to market.
The heroism of the unheroic.
I don't understand his patience.
How can I sing about patience?'

'He does whatever the task demands.
I don't have the patience
translates *I don't care.*'

'But you can't write a praise song
for administrators.' He giggled.

'He'd rather read documents
than slaughter his enemies.
Rather check his accounts
than go to a wedding.

He encouraged families
to live in watch towers
and within ruined towns.
He rebuilt city walls.
He maintained the roads.

Deathless poetry.'
He refilled his cup.

'Even his new field army isn't worth a song.
It's monotonously successful.
They ride. They fight. They slaughter.
No raiding party has a chance.
I can't compose songs about them.
He is killing the bards of Britain.'

'If Merlin's right about his son,
you'll be singing about him 'til the end of time.'

'But you, with your magic and princes
and most beautiful of women.
Why don't you write about normal?
It's not like you don't know it.
You're as comfortable in the shepherd's hut
or pig keeper's shack as you are at court.
You know every stable boy and serving maid
ploughman and priest, farmer and forester
cheese maker and cook, seamstress and sailor,
poacher and prostitute from sea to shining sea.
Why don't you put them in "a story"?'

'Who'd listen if I did?'

'A story where people treated each other
as they'd like to be treated.'

'I don't do fairy tales.'

'I tried an honest war song once.
Your challenge, remember?
Didn't polish it but I'm drunk enough to hope
we'll both forget it in the morning.[39]

Did he saddle his horse before the sun rose,
stung by the cold, while the shivering torches
flicked long shadows on the stockade walls?

Did his hands shake checking his harness,
watched by proud elders, whispering siblings?
Was there refuge in detail? Did the tearful maid,

tangle his thoughts as he rode through the gate?
Old men compared scars, repeating their stories,
hiding the horror so boys become warriors.

---

[39] As there is no poem like this in the historical poems, no attempt has been made to copy any of the metrical patterns used by the historical Taliesin.

The hero scorns death, dies laughing,
protecting his fame. Preposterous tales,
polished as heirlooms, handed down,

prophylactics against doubt. And was there doubt
in the rider's banter, on the straight road to battle?
Did he boast with his friends of the deeds they'd perform?

Did he pay for his mead with the blood in his veins?
Did his training suffice? Did he conquer his fear?
Did his sword strike sparks from his enemies' steel?

Did he beg for the life he had not lived
as the spear pushed home? As the blade slashed down?
What was he thinking when his comrades fled;

left him to die, to bleed out alone,
watching the ravens, watching him, waiting,
before their beaks hooked into still open eyes?

Did she work with her parents, watching the road?
How long did she hope, with stragglers returning?
Did she remember his face, in the years remaining

in another man's hut, in his arms, in his bed?
Watching her children, did she ever consider
what kind of father that boy might have been?

Old men in winter, shun the fire's warmth,
sit by the door, still watching the road,
for sons to return from last spring's raid.

I forget the rest.
Who'd want to hear it?'

3

'Father,' cried the boy, knocking the books from the table.
Uther, laughing, lifted him so they were face to face.

Years ago they'd watched him manoeuvring toy soldiers.
'You've done a good job, Gwydion.
These other boys, bind them to him.
As adults they will share his plunder and his grief.'

'He's burning through his teachers.
His Latin's good. I've taught him Saxon.
He's read the books you sent.
And since your Gallic priest arrived,
they're working through the Gospels.'

The stories he had told him,
were versions told for her.
The stag inside the boy,
educated into consciousness.

Now, ten years later, they watch the same young men
training with swords. 'He's good,' says Uther.

The land has been at peace.
They say a woman with a baby at her breast,
or a merchant with his bag of gold,
can walk the island unmolested.
He has mastered the unspectacular,
unheroic art of organising his kingdom
but will not live to fear his son's ambition.

Owain Rheged is dead.
The bards extemporise their elegies
but Taliesin's is the one on everybody's lips
and Gwydion is delighted for his friend.
Urien is being smothered,

pushed south by the inexorable,
creeping accumulation of Saxons.

'Hengist's sons are on the run.
Did they turn themselves to water
and flow through the locks of their cells?
Easier to believe than that a watchful man
looking to his future
might dabble in betrayal?'

'I'd heard they've gone north
to submit to Colgrim,
who's landed another army.'

One more push along the great north road.
You can fight the waves;
you can't hold back the tide.
Uther the Maimed King
taking leave of a friend.

'I sent Lot, but the lords won't follow him.
They're making deals with Colgrim
forgetting no one dances with the Devil
and escapes damnation.

I never stopped asking.
Merlin insists he had no part in it.
He's waiting to play chief councillor.
Look after my son. He will offer him
everything he shouldn't have.'

'Of course. The queen is well?'

'Time refines her beauty and sharpens her mind.
When I die, she'll rule until he's old enough
and heaven help anyone who crosses her
or threatens him.'

'Gwydion,' said Arthur, after Uther had gone,
'you don't like my mother, do you?
Please don't start another story.
You are only formal with my father
when you mention her. I'm surprised
you don't break into Latin.'

'You don't miss much, do you?'

'When I am king, I will order you to tell me.'

'When you are king, my son,
I will answer any question you ask,
which is in my power to answer, And which…'
            'Yes, yes. You taught me the qualifications.'

They watched the royal banners disappear into the distance.
'My father says there never will be peace
unless the country is united.
He says, reward achievement,
encourage effort, punish disobedience.
When I am king, I will devise a way
so that those who would gain most from anarchy
devote their lives to fighting it.
The holy man says, I was hungry…'

'I know that passage well.
I've heard your father quote it many times.'

'I will harness the Church to my cause.
I will make them convince the people
that heaven will be their reward,
and hell their punishment.

I will make people swear to help the weak and poor,
and never harm a woman, regardless of her rank.

I will make them believe that fighting for peace and justice
is preferable to the selfishness that leads to war.'[40]

'Good luck with that.
And what will you do with your enemies?
What will you do with those
keen to take advantage of your kindness?'

'Is this a trick question? A riddle? No?
I will annihilate them.
I will make the thought of opposition unthinkable,
and loyalty the only road to profit.

Loyalty to an ideal, not the individual,
the office, not the incumbent.'

That will make a fine story, thought Gwydion,
about the tragic failure of a noble experiment.

4

Urien Rheged, outside Uther's tent
talking with the guards.
Orphan boys Uther had raised,
who owed him everything,
and saw him as the uncomplicated father
of a young boy's dreams. Older
than he was when he first decided
to follow the dragon banner.

Old men who claim that they have no regrets
are delusional or amnesiac.
But he remembers knowing,

---

[40] This is not Laȝamon's Arthur. From 'I will make them swear …to …war' is essentially the oath Malory's Round Table Knights swear each Pentecost.

immediately, that Uther
was the man to follow.

A sturdy woman carries water
between the rows of tents.
Two small children trotting to keep up.
The smallest, on still rebellious legs,
moves in a stutter of half-controlled accidents.

The loss of wife and son were scars on his life.
Uther's death will snuff the sun out
and the bards will be dumb
at the end of the world.

He is waiting for the doctors' verdict.
Poison? They mutter and shrug.
He's been ill so long it's no longer possible
to identify what's killing him.
Anyone else would have died years ago.

How many times
has he stepped into a space like this,
before or after how many battles?
The table with the maps.
The armour on its stand.

In such a space the messenger had whispered,
'The Lady Ness is dead'
emptying the moment of all other sound.
Like a spear through a stone slab
slamming into Uther Pendragon.
Where poison, point and edge had failed
five softly spoken words prevailed.
His friend became the Maimed King,
driven through the wasting years
by duty and his sense of obligation.

Uther is lying on a camp bed.
A corpse faced bundle of bones
laid out for his coffin.
He tries to rise. 'Well?'

'Hengist's sons.
No Colgrim. No Badulf.
They still outnumber us.
The rise is in their favour.'

'Shield wall my arse.
It's not a shield wall,
it's a line of nervous men
holding wooden boards.
Most of them are hoping
we'll turn and run for home.'

When body won't cooperate,
mind remains. And that,
now, is what he needs.

Propped on his friend,
he can see the line
on the other side of the valley:
a dark ragged hedge.

'What idiot leaves his flanks exposed like that?
Send squadrons of horse archers to harry them.'

'Britannia?'

    'Of course.
Have I told you about the best day of my life?'

'Once or twice.'

'Aetius would look at them and laugh:
That's not an army: it's a mob with weapons.
Atilla would be wondering why they want to die today.
Let them wait. We'll see if their nerve holds.
Put me on my horse. Unfurl the royal standard,
show my army, Uther, their king, is with them.'

'The doctors say that will definitely kill you.'

'I was the best horseman they'd ever seen.
When their lines broke, I chased mad Thorismund
all the way into Attila's camp. Huns everywhere,
but I got to him. Grabbed that lunatic's bridle,
and turning him round, raced back to our lines
in the dark. Best rider they'd ever seen.
That's what the Huns said. Now Merlin says
my son will be the greatest of the British Kings.
But there's stiff competition for that title.

In the morning all the riderless horses,
drifting over the plain,
or standing where their masters died,
waiting patiently for them to rise again.
Half a million dead men and it solved nothing.
We didn't even know who'd won.

Only once or twice?'

'A week.'

The army is an animal chanting his name;
a terrible two syllable exhalation.
He rides along their front,
with the golden dragon
snapping and flapping in his wake,
speaking to the remembered faces,
stopping to talk with a man

who fought for him at Dunian.
He explains what they must do.

The Saxons tense, then
as their nerve breaks,
the wave bursts round and over them.

When they bring the news:
the line is broken;
the enemy in flight;
victory is theirs,
Uther is already dead.

They say that at his funeral,
even his horses wept.

La3amon's Last Interview

A tiny grey stone hut cramped
on the green edge of a wide,
bleached estuary. The window slit squints
to the thin rumpled line of distant sea.
Tide out, the mudflats ribboned
by bright threads of shallow water shiver
with moving flocks of wading birds.
There is nothing to stop the wind
bounding over the flats to bully the shingle roof.
In the shelter of its wall, cleaning
a cauldron that hangs from a tripod,
a woman tends a miraculous fire.
Her long black hair, streaked white,
tugged loose to misbehave
by the eddying clutch of the wind.

A grey horse blurred by two great wolfhounds
flowing towards her from the ford.
She watches the rider with suspicion:
spears, battle axe, sword, and shield.
Then she notices the purple cloak,
the golden brooch. At his command,
the dogs drop. Gwydion dismounts
and greets her, courteously.

'Father', piercing the wind's rummage,
'there's a Welsh lord here to see you.'
From inside an excited voice scrabbling:
'Gerald? I heard that you were dead.'
The old priest shambles towards the door
'til disappointment staggers him.
The woman grabs his arm,
helps him back towards his bed.

Gwydion, stooping to enter,
'You're a hard man to find.'

'I didn't know anyone was looking.'

The woman blocks the doorway;
her shadow and the priest,
two darker stains on the rough wall.

One stool, one bed, two bowls,
two wooden spoons.
No books. No writing materials.
He can taste the damp.

'She looks after me.
I don't know why.'

'Because you need looking after.
Don't wind him up, sir, please.
He's a bugger to settle.'

'The Lateran council forbade the priest his wife or concubine.
Gerald made the usual Latin puns so few could understand.
But why shouldn't a man hold someone in the dark?
And how could I survive without her patient charity?'

'They called you latimer, not priest.'

'I translate at those sad times
m'lord shouts at his tenants
and they need to understand
or when he's threatened
by the written word.

You're Welsh? Kyuarwydd?[41]

---

[41] A storyteller or professional entertainer but also one who knows, who is well known, one who is well versed in magic or, in this case, all of those.

A professional storyteller.
Trained in the tradition.
Valued. Honoured.
How very easy for you.
How very lucrative.'

'You know as well as I,
no one stands on the summit
who hasn't sweated the slopes.
I read your history.
I liked it very much.'

'You must be the only man who has.'

'You wrote in English.
Did you expect an audience to rival Monmouth's?'

The woman interrupts.
'They feed us, bread, cheese, honey.
Sometimes meat and wine if he's been useful.
I'd offer you some but there's nothing in the pot.'

'You should be proud of it; your history.'

'See,' she says, 'you did a great thing.
I've heard about his book.
When he's in a good mood,
he tells me stories from it.'

'It was a job. I did my best.
What more is there?'

'God knows it was much more than that.
All those years you spent,
moving stories from one language
to another. Adding, expanding,
explaining. A line of French blossoms

into a speech. A place name flowers
into dramatic battle music.
I have a question: what did you learn?'

No one has ever asked him this.

'Only fools waste time writing?'

'When I read your story
I see a world where everyone has a role.
King, Queen, Bishop, Knight.
The noun becomes a verb.
There are no individuals,
just good, better, best.
Is that what you believe?'

'I believe in God the Maker.
But He's asleep and doesn't care
for me, or anybody else.
Why must a story have designs upon its audience?
It's the only form of lying
for which no penance is required.'

Promising to return,
Gwydion steps into the wind
wondering why she chooses to live here,
where the stench of wasted talent
is more lethal than the damp.

The blue-eyed wonder boy,
the man most likely to,
reduced to a bitter skull
perched on a pile of rags.
What terrible hinge of fate
refused to open on the future
everyone thought was his?

2

The light slabs off the water
in a broken, blinding dazzle.
Yesterday's labyrinth of sandbanks
marked by ripples on the surface.
The priest sits by the door,
eyes closed, face turned towards the sun.

Two dead rabbits. 'For the pot', said Gwydion,
then placed a bag of silver pennies
on the scored plank she was using as a table.

'What did I learn?
History is the failed teacher of a repetitious lesson?
Those with too much, always wanting more,
take from those with precious left to lose.
That's hardly news.
What do you think life means, storyteller?
Greater minds than ours have shipwrecked on that question.
Do you think wind and sky and sea worry about meaning?

History like the Severn flowing past my church;
in raging flood and creeping stillness,
tumbling the sordid and the beautiful.
Everything words separate and value,
rolled together on the passing years.
Is that news? I doubt it.

I have seen the great names of the age:
Henry the high king, and Eleanor his queen,
Richard, John, poor baffled Henry,
Gerald, Map, William the Marshall
and that other William surrounded by his books
 in Malmesbury's scriptorium.

And which of them was better than the snivelling boy
who held my horse the first day I arrived at Areley,
or this woman who gave me shelter
when I was lost, alone and very scared?'

'Malmesbury died before you were born.'

'There was a great man.
He'd answer your question.
I struggle to remember Henry.
Sometimes I doubt I ever saw him.'

'You're a long way down your river.
I asked for you there.
They remember you with fondness and respect.'

'Twenty-five years, plodding the parish.
Doing my best for the people in my care.'

'Isn't that something?
To be so good at what you did
they still remember you
as somebody who changed their lives?'

'Fondness doesn't get your work read.
I watched as lesser talents won the prizes and the praise.
I knew I had done something no one else had done
and instead of recognition, silence.'

'We've all sung that song.
You believe that God the Maker hibernates
while Fortune spins her wheel
and you're surprised that talent's unrewarded?'

'Areley was temporary!
"Wait there until it's safe,"
they said. "We'll send for you,"

they said. 25 years I waited.
Great men have no memory
for those who cannot help or harm.'

'The new priest looks over his shoulder
dreading your return.'

'I have the estuary,
Ceridwen's company,
bird song for music.

Old bones won't travel far.
Tired eyes don't see to read.
I close them
and remember Britain.

The mind moves if the body won't
along the paths I used to travel.
The world is a beautiful place.
I am at home in four languages,
and no words do it justice.
Is that in my book? I doubt it.'

Gwydion waits, but the old man has shut his eyes.
The tide is coming in. The causeway flooding.
He will have to go the long way round.
He rises but the priest resumes,
snatching at his cloak. 'Perhaps.

Perhaps I learnt there will be another day like this:
the wind battering whatever's in its way;
clouds like a crumbling wall on the horizon,
the sea beating time against the shore.
And wind and sea and sky won't notice that we're gone.

A thousand years ago your country was invaded,
your homes were stolen, your language

and your culture all but disappeared.
Two hundred years ago mine was destroyed.[42]
Too bad. We lost. Get over it.
What good is history if it only bleats;
It's not our fault we're like this now,
don't judge us, we were greater. Once.'

Gwydion shakes himself free.
Ceridwen follows him outside.

'Arglwydd,' she says,
her hand on the horse's bridle,
'this is not who he is.
He turns nasty
when someone successful
reminds him that he failed.'

'In which of his four languages
could that word apply?
He made Britain English.
He sang a landscape into being.'

'In which of them does this define success?
How nice to be remembered with affection.
Affection won't put food in the pot.
What good's the world's applause
for something you don't value?

You know he risked his life,
travelling alone, on foot,
when it was open season on the clergy,
for a story in a shepherd's hut,
or a book that might be in a library?

Years when he danced
to the music of creation,

---

[42] La3amon's poem suggests he wasn't good with numbers.

listened, wrote and read
looking at this world
through the stained-glass window
of his imagination.
Drunk with the pleasure
he walked his fields
with the mighty dead.

Then they were gone.
Leaving only Areley
and a god that never responds.

Reminds me of a sailor I once met.
Hard travelling on the long haul out,
risking death or disappointment
to arrive at the unexpected miracle
only to discover that he couldn't stay.

Left with a memory
that measures everything
and proves it wanting.

Now he's dying,
and every morning
is another insult.'

'We are not rivers, trees, or rocks.
We are the animal that narrates,
in need of storytellers
to remind us there's a path through the trees,
and home is somewhere we are free to reimagine.

I have a wife, estates, an audience,
things he's never had.
My stories are a voice
in the clatter of the feast.
The drinkers at the benches

don't return from battle.
The language that I love
is heard from fewer mouths.
We are smoke on the breeze.

But centuries from now,
when we're as distant from those people
as Brutus is to us,
someone will read his stories
and all those characters
who lived inside his head
will be alive again.

A life we can't imagine
will be altered by the words he wrote.
Surely that's a miracle
even the Devil won't dispute?'

'Not much good to him now, sir, is it?'

www.ingramcontent.com/pod-product-compliance
Lightning Source LLC
Chambersburg PA
CBHW022011160426
43197CB00007B/384